At-Home Activities for Reading, Language Arts, and Social Studies

Over 100 Activities to Increase Children's Love of Learning

by
Robyn Freedman Spizman
and
Marianne Daniels Garber, Ph.D.

illustrated by Janet Armbrust

Cover by Teresa Mathis

Copyright © 1994, Good Apple

ISBN No. 0-86653-817-8

Printing No. 9876543

Good Apple
A Division of Frank Schaffer Publications, Inc.
23740 Hawthorne Boulevard
Torrance, CA 90505-5927

Dear Parents and Teachers:

At-Home Activities is a new series of teaching aids designed to offer you a wonderful opportunity to enhance your students' learning experiences by bridging home and school. *At-Home Activities* was created to unite home and school by utilizing the myriad of teaching opportunities that are available during the normal activities parents undertake at home.

In *At-Home Activities for Reading, Language Arts, and Social Studies,* you will find that everyday experiences and common knowledge are utilized to spur the child to learn something new or reinforce a principle taught at school. From the kitchen to art room and outdoors, a variety of activities is suggested for the parent to use with little preparation.

Everyday activities become the basis for creative learning in all the subject areas, not just reading, language arts, and social studies. Each activity has a wide range of applications and enhances learning. In real life, learning is not isolated by subject. Although each activity focuses on one skill in reading, language arts, and social studies, each exercise also complements other subject areas.

For example, "Be an Ad Watcher" on page 35 is a social studies activity and language arts activity. The child first cuts out five advertisements and identifies what is being sold. When you read the ad and have the child identify descriptive words, you expand language use. Having the child draw his or her own ad provides an opportunity to creatively use language for a purpose. The child becomes a critical thinker as he or she evaluates price and selects reasons someone might want to purchase an object.

To enhance your child's learning experience:
1. Complete the activity as designed.
2. Get down on the child's level when you do the activity.
3. Praise your child's participation with specific feedback. "I like the way you carefully observed what was happening." "That's an interesting idea; what happens when you do this. . . ?" "Yes, you identified all the descriptive words. . . . "
4. Listen carefully to your child. Repeat his or her comments to encourage him or her to share more ideas. Give your child time to think and answer. In addition, say, "Yes, that's a good idea; tell me more," providing another opportunity for him or her to share information.
5. Apply other basic skills such as labeling, counting, comparing, identifying beginning and end sounds, and describing. Always ask what else your child can do with the object or game. You will be surprised by the answer.

Most importantly, *At-Home Activities* makes learning and homework fun. It adds a new twist to an age-old task. *At-Home Activities* allows the parent to become involved in meaningful activities to enhance learning as the child finds that homework can be interesting, entertaining, and informative.

At-Home Activities is meant for the family and child to do together. In this way family members can easily assume their roles in providing hands-on support for the learning that occurs each day. As they become naturally more involved in what their children learn, the child benefits from the family involvement, support, and interest.

Families and kids alike will think *At-Home Activities* is fun, as they team up to make homework one of the best parts of their day together.

Happy homework!
Robyn Freedman Spizman and Marianne Daniels Garber, Ph.D.

GA1509

Reading and Language Arts

IMAGINATION · LISTENING · MESSAGES · ABC's · STORYTELLING · CREATIVITY · PICTURES · VERBAL SKILLS · WRITING · SENTENCES

GA1509

Out-of-Doors

At-Home Objective: Encourage your child's verbal skills and build language skills by labeling the environment.

Activity: As you take a walk with your child, talk about what you see around you. Label the things you see. When you return home have your child draw a picture about one thing he or she saw on the walk. Ask him or her to tell you a sentence about his or her picture and write it in block letters under the picture.

GA1509

Alphabet Search

At-Home Objective:	Use this activity to reinforce alphabet letters.
Activity:	Have your child search for things that begin with any of the letters found in his or her first name. List the words on this page, placing each one under the correct letter.

Write the letters found in your name here.

___ ___ ___ ___ ___ ___ ___ ___ ___ ___ ___ ___

GA1509

ABCs and Me!

At-Home Objective: Use this activity to reinforce the alphabet.

Activity: Show that you know your ABCs and list a noun for each letter
                               of the alphabet.

A apple
B Bear
C cat
D Doll
E Elephant
F Fish
G Giraffe
H House
I Iguana
J
K
L
M
N
O
P
Q
R
S
T
U
V
W
X
Y
Z

4

GA1509

I Can Find It

At-Home Objective: Use this activity to teach letter recognition and build observation skills.

Activity: Ask your child to find particular letters of the alphabet on food cartons and cans. For example, can you find three *A*s and two *T*s on the soup cans? Can you find five *S*s and five *O*s on the cereal boxes? Have your child keep a tally of the number of letters he or she finds.

5

GA1509

Follow the Leader

At-Home Objective: Help your child identify beginning sounds of words. Learning to discriminate beginning consonant sounds is an important reading skill.

Activity: Play follow the leader as you take a journey around the house following the leader. The leader makes different motions and also calls out a letter. The next person in line must identify a nearby object that begins with that letter.

GA1509

ABCs of Cooking

At-Home Objective: The kitchen is a natural place for learning experiences. You spend a lot of time in the kitchen so your child does too. You can use your pantry for a variety of learning experiences if you don't mind a little mess. This activity teaches letter recognition.

Activity: Take ten cans of food that have pictures on the labels from the pantry. Identify the beginning letter of each food. Write each letter on an index card and place the cards on the floor.

With a nonreader, underline the first letter of the food with a red marker. Instruct your child to say the underlined letter and place the can on the matching index card.

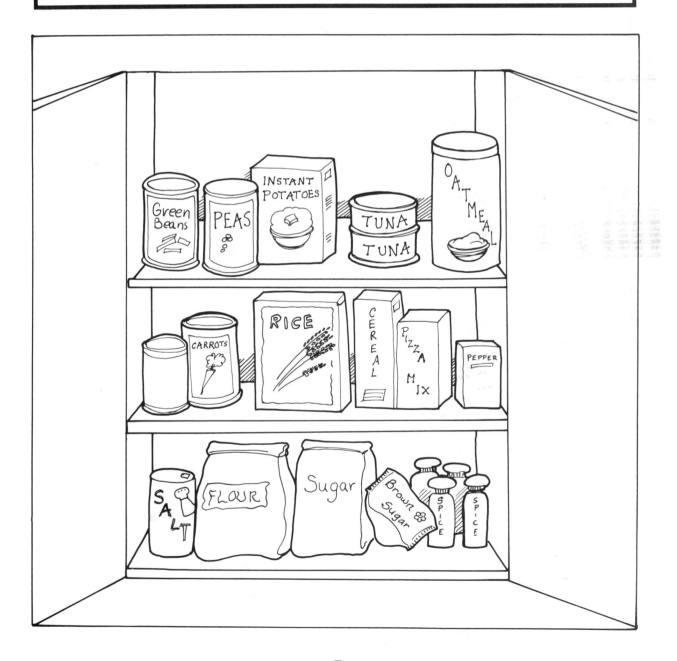

GA1509

Alphabet Soup

B	S	C
I	D	P
A	R	J
T	O	G

8

Guess What It Is!

At-Home Objective: This game reinforces sound discrimination and can be played at home, in a restaurant, or while you are waiting anywhere.

Activity: Play a guessing game. Tell your child that you are thinking of the name of something you see in the kitchen. You will give a clue to the word by supplying a word that rhymes with it. For example, if the mystery item is a broom, you might say, "room."

What's the Word Search?

At-Home Objective: Use this activity for practicing and encouraging alphabetizing skills.

Activity: Search for the words listed in this word search, and each time you find one circle it. Once you have found all ten words, put them in alphabetical order.

Words to Look For

carrot   cheese
cake   long
people   puppies
smile   large
write   letter

B C A R R O T Q P Z A
I H U L V V E U E V R
G E R S M I L E O G T
S E V L A R G E P H I
H S J S T E V E L A S
A E A L A C A K E R F
L A N E B L Q M N A U
L M E T C O P N S O E
W R I T E N R M B R U
O A T E B G S T S A M
W Q B R P U P P I E S

List the words in alphabetical order.

1. cake
2. carrot
3. cheese
4. large
5. letter

6. long
7. peole
8. puppies
9. write
10. _____

10

GA1509

Go on a Word Search

Words to Look For
List ten spelling words of your choice.

1. _____
2. _____
3. _____
4. _____
5. _____
6. _____
7. _____
8. _____
9. _____
10. _____

K I T T E N S

List the words in alphabetical order.

1. _____
2. _____
3. _____
4. _____
5. _____

6. _____
7. _____
8. _____
9. _____
10. _____

11

A, B, C, and Me

At-Home Objective: Once a child knows the alphabet and letters, there are many opportunities at your fingertips to teach alphabetical order.

Activity: Put ten cans of food on the floor. With your child, identify each food item. Have the child write the first letter he or she hears in the word on an index card and then arrange the cards in alphabetical order by first and second letters. Next have the child arrange the cans in the same order.

Write the letters in the cans below.

GA1509

A Year at a Glance

Simon Says

At-Home Objective: Use this activity to encourage good listening habits and following directions.

Activity: Simon says to follow these directions!

1. Draw a line under the clown.
2. Circle the flower.
3. Put the letter *B* on the bunny.
4. Draw a hat on the turtle.
5. Draw a square around the present.
6. Put an *X* on top of the telephone.

GA1509

Stop, Look, and Listen

At-Home Objective: Use this activity to encourage your child's ability to follow directions.

Activity: Follow these directions and complete the picture with your colorful touch.

1. Color the clown's costume yellow.
2. Color the clown's hat, smile, and nose red.
3. Color the clown's buttons blue.
4. Color the balls the clown is juggling green.
5. Color the clown's cheeks pink.

15

GA1509

What's the Story?

At-Home Objective: Use this activity to reinforce sequencing and good listening skills.

Activity: Read the story below and cut out the pictures and put them in the right order.

Sally went to the circus.
She bought a balloon.
She ate cotton candy.

GA1509

Secret Message

At-Home Objective: Use this activity to reinforce recognition skills and to build listening and spelling skills.

Activity: Send your child a secret message. Call out the letters of a message one letter at a time. Each time your child finds the letter on an item in the pantry, have him or her write the letters down below in the order called. When your child is finished, the letters should spell a hidden message.

My Secret

17

GA1509

Reading Time

At-Home Objective: Build listening skills and story sense.

Activity: Read your child's favorite story and stop reading, asking him or her to supply the next word or tell you a new ending for the story. Have your child draw a picture of the new word in the book.

GA1509

ABC Away

At-Home Objective: Use this game to improve listening skills and to build auditory memory skills.

Activity:

Name a letter of the alphabet.

Start a sentence "I am going to _____ " with a place that begins with the identified letter. Walk around the house and take turns adding items to take on the trip that begin with the same letter.

What would be on your list if you were going to Brazil?

Play variations of this game in the car or while waiting for your food at a restaurant. Begin with the consonants; later use blends and vowels.

19

GA1509

Paper Dolls

At-Home Objective: Use this game to increase your child's sight vocabulary.

Activity: Have your child use the words listed to label the correct clothing items on each paper doll.

jacket	collar
blouse	belt
pants	skirt
shoes	hat
socks	scarf

GA1509

What Else Can It Do?

At-Home Objective: Most objects have more than one use. Children are often very rigid in their thinking. Encourage your child to be more flexible by asking him or her to think of all the ways a common object can be used.

Activity:

1. Show your child a brick. Ask him or her to think of all the ways a brick might be used (building material, paperweight, hammer, tombstone for a small animal).

2. Talk about the new ways common objects are shown in the picture. Show your child a plate. Ask him or her to draw another way the plate might be used besides for eating.

21

GA1509

Comfy Conversation Starters

At-Home Objective: Use this activity to practice language skills and expand vocabulary.

Activity: Use these conversation starters as you drive in the car or take a walk.

What do you think squirrels do for fun?

The leaves on the trees are _____. Can you tell what season it is? What happens during this time of year?

What would it be like if it were dark in the daytime and light at night?

Let's pretend we are on our way to the _____. What do you want to do when we get there? Draw a picture about it, and then tell me where you want to go.

GA1509

Guess What It Is!

At-Home Objective: Encourage your child to expand his or her vocabulary with new descriptive words.

Activity: Ask your child to fill a paper bag with three small objects but not to tell you what they are. One at a time, without showing you what's in the bag or using any object's name, have the child describe an object. See if you can guess it from the description. Switch roles, and describe your surprise objects so that your child can guess each one.

Add the descriptive words you and your child use to the bags below.

WAXY

SCRATCHY

GOOEY   SOFT

SMALL

23

GA1509

Pop Up a Puppet

At-Home Objective: Encourage your child to use language by talking through a puppet.

Activity:

1. Gather two brown paper bags, glue, scissors, construction paper, and crayons.

2. Help your child make a paper bag puppet of an animal you might see on a walk, as you make your own puppet. You may trace the form below for the head of a cat or dog, or draw your own form.

3. Talk to your child through the puppet. First introduce yourselves using pretend voices. Identify the animals' names and what they like to do. Have a pretend snack together and talk about what you do all day.

← MOUTH

GA1509

Phone Memory

At-Home Objective: Auditory and visual memory are important skills for social studies and other subjects. Help your child learn tricks to remembering things.

Activity: Have your child pretend to take a photograph of his or her telephone number. Write the telephone number in large numerals below. Have your child study the number, "take a picture" of it with his or her mind, and write the number three times on the telephones below.

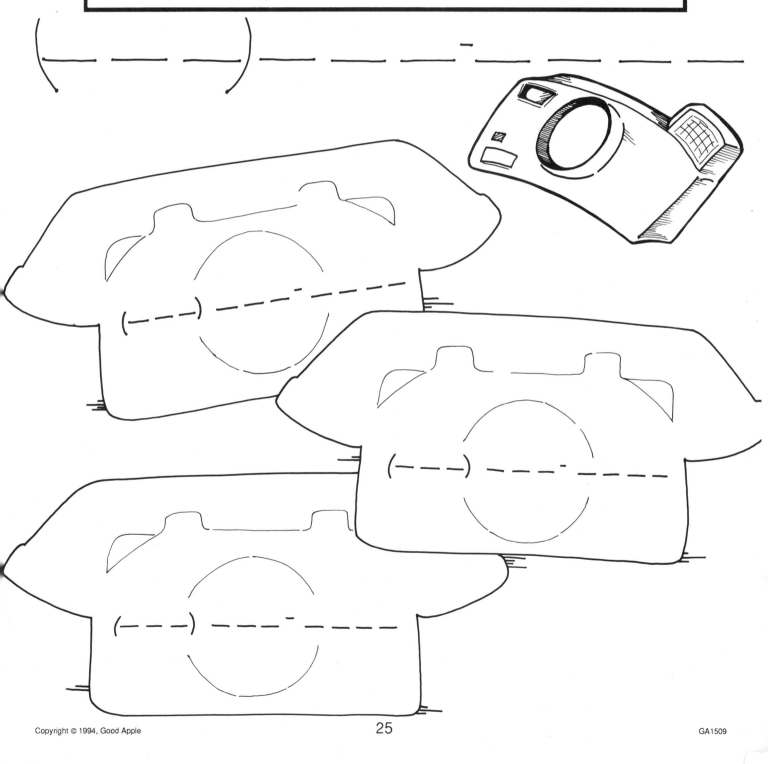

25

GA1509

Lights On, Lights Off

At-Home Objective: Use these activities to teach your child the concept of opposites.

Activity:

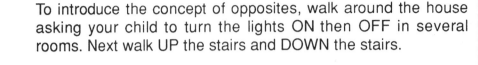

To introduce the concept of opposites, walk around the house asking your child to turn the lights ON then OFF in several rooms. Next walk UP the stairs and DOWN the stairs.

Have your child give you the opposite of several words, such as *on, up, little, fast*, etc.

Ask your child to write the word or tell you the word to complete each pair of opposites in the boxes below.

big	
fast	
full	
fat	
tall	
light	

26

GA1509

Who Is First?

At-Home Objective: Reinforce your child's sequencing skills with this activity.

Activity: Read the sentence and then number the pictures 1, 2, 3, 4, and put them in the correct order.

My mom asked me to set the table.

GA1509

Comic Relief

At-Home Objective: Use this activity to help your child learn to sequence the events of a story.

Activity: Choose a comic strip and cut it apart. Try to put it back together and glue it on this page in the correct order.

28

Cut It Out!

At-Home Objective: Use this activity to encourage your child to make complete sentences.

Activity: Cut out a variety of words from the newspaper and place them in an envelope. Challenge your child to select words from the envelope, put them in order, and glue them below to make complete sentences.

29

GA1509

Comic Stories

At-Home Objective: Teach your child to put stories in sequence.

Activity: After your family has read the Sunday paper, help your child cut out some of his or her favorite comic strips. Using one comic strip at a time, have your child cut the strip into its windows. Mix them up and arrange them in an order that makes sense.

GA1509

Scrambled Eggs

At-Home Objective: Cooking offers the perfect opportunity to create sequences. Create recipes, and give your child practice in putting actions into the correct order.

Activity: Talk about the steps you must take to make scrambled eggs, pour a bowl of cereal, make a cheese sandwich, or an ice-cream sundae. Have your child dictate a recipe for one of the items he or she can make. Using the recipe card, print the ingredients, utensils, and then the instructions in the exact order dictated by your child.

Try out the recipe as it is written. There will probably be some funny results! Let your child correct the directions and start again. Enjoy your creation!

FROM _____'s KITCHEN

INGREDIENTS:

DIRECTIONS:

GA1509

Room to Room

At-Home Objective: Use this activity to help your child learn how to categorize and identify verbs.

Activity:

1. Walk through the rooms in your house with your child. Talk about what kinds of things people *do* in each room. Explain that the word that tells what people *do* is called a verb.

2. On the house below, write for your child or have your child write several verbs that describe actions that occur in each room. Suggest that your child draw a picture of something he or she likes to do in each room.

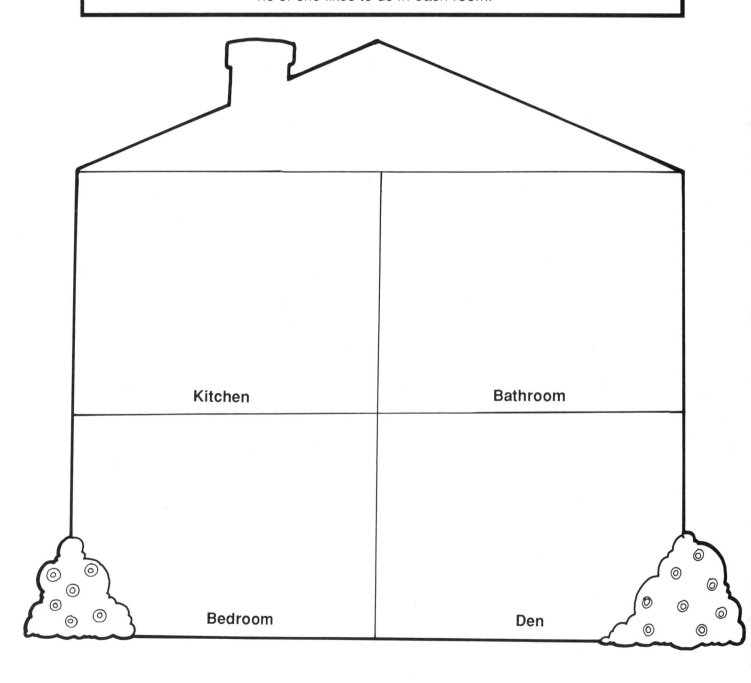

Kitchen

Bathroom

Bedroom

Den

GA1509

On the Farm

At-Home Objective: Use this activity to help your child use thinking skills and clues to figure out the answers.

Activity: Make each animal talk by writing the correct sound next to it.

Sounds: moo; peep, peep; oink, oink; meow; bow wow; baaaa; neigh

33

GA1509

Zoo Who?

At-Home Objective: Reinforce your child's thinking and visual perception skills with this activity.

Activity: Color everything that you would find at the zoo.

34

GA1509

Be an Ad Watcher

At-Home Objective: Use this activity to improve your child's thinking skills.

Activity:

1. Have your child cut out five full-page ads from magazines. Look at each very carefully. Answer the questions:
   What is the ad trying to sell?
   What pictures does it use to make you like the product?
   What words describe the product?

2. Have your child design his or her own ad for a favorite restaurant, toy, or movie.

GA1509

To the Editor

At-Home Objective: Use this activity to build critical thinking skills and the ability to express one's opinion.

Activity: Show your child the Letters to the Editor page of the newspaper. Discuss that one right of citizenship is to express an opinion. Look for an issue that affects children, and have your child write a letter to the appropriate official.

Use the letter form below to teach your child the correct format for a business letter.

Date: _____

Name: _____

Title: _____

Address: _____

_____

Dear _____,

_____

_____

_____

_____

_____

_____

_____

Sincerely,

_____

GA1509

Disappearing Letters

At-Home Objective: Practice letter-writing skills and recognition.

Activity:
Warning: This is a fun but messy activity!
Give your child a large sheet of **waxed paper** and a dish of chocolate pudding. Spread some chocolate pudding on the page. For the younger child, write a letter of the alphabet and have him or her trace it. Otherwise call out the letters. Your child will love this activity.

GA1509

Contraction Action

At-Home Objective: Use this activity to reinforce your child's understanding of contractions.

Activity: Match the contraction with its correct mate. Draw a line connecting them.

GA1509

First Class Mistakes!

At-Home Objective: Use this activity to reinforce your child's visual perception and ability to pay attention to details.

Activity: Search for the mistakes on this page and once you find them, put circles around them. Complete the picture by coloring the rest of it.

39

GA1509

Are You Mistaken?

At-Home Objective: Use this activity to reinforce your child's visual awareness.

Activity: Take a good look at this picture and see if you can find ten mistakes. Color all of the things that are either out of place or don't belong in this picture.

GA1509

Upsy-Daisy

At-Home Objective: Increase thinking skills by playing common games with the rules reversed.

Activity:

1. Use the board to play tic-tac-toe a new way. Three *X*s or *O*s in a row loses.

2. Play Simon Says, but only do what Simon says when the leader doesn't say, "Simon says, . . ."

3. Play Monopoly™, but the first player to lose all his or her money wins!

41

GA1509

Sentence Sense

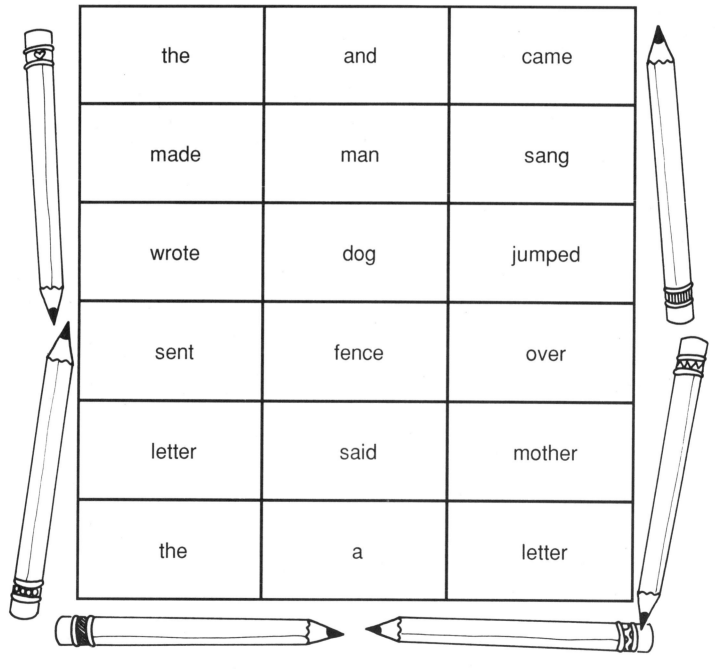

the	and	came
made	man	sang
wrote	dog	jumped
sent	fence	over
letter	said	mother
the	a	letter

girl	played	at
park	ran	school
cake	in	climbed
cat	barked	tree
went	to	song
note	town	me
is	here	they

43

GA1509

Sentence Machine

At-Home Objective: Help your child become familiar with the parts of sentences by unscrambling words to make new sentences. Use the sentence machine to get your child revved up to make sense out of these scrambled words.

Activity: Label a shoe box as a sentence machine. Cut an opening wide enough for 3" x 5" (7.62 x 12.7 cm) cards to fit through the slot. Make up sentences appropriate for your child's level of reading. Cut the sentences into separate words. Paper clip each group of words together.

Have your child select a group of words to put into the sentence machine. Your child draws each card out of the machine and combines the cards to make a sentence.

44

Make Your Mark
(Bookmark, That Is!)

At-Home Objective: Use this activity as a creative writing exercise to show your child's understanding of a favorite book.

Activity: Make a creative bookmark that illustrates a favorite book that you have read.

GA1509

Smart Work

At-Home Objective: Use this activity to encourage reading by putting your child's reading skills to work.

Activity:

1. Select a place in your city that your child would like to visit, such as the zoo, capitol, a museum, or a sports stadium. Get a city map, bus route, or subway map and plan the route you will take to get to the place. Have your child identify the mode of transportation, the route, and the time it will take to get there on the form below.

2. Have your child look up the phone number of the place in the telephone book; then call to find out how much the entrance fee is and what times the place is open.

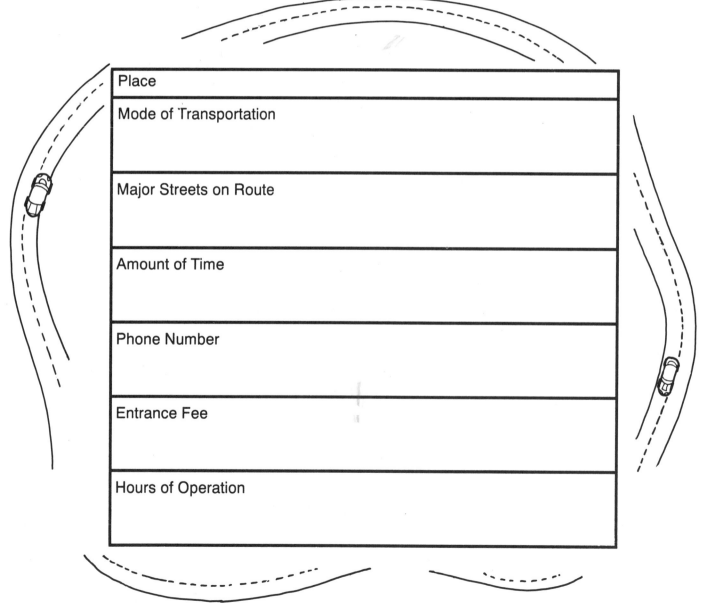

Place
Mode of Transportation
Major Streets on Route
Amount of Time
Phone Number
Entrance Fee
Hours of Operation

GA1509

Signs of the Times

At-Home Objective: Increase your child's sight vocabulary with this activity.

Activity: Before leaving for a ride, give your child the pictures of street signs below. Read each sign together. As you drive, have your child identify every time he or she sees one of the signs. How many times did he or she see each sign?

47

GA1509

Now You See It

At-Home Objective: To provide practice in sight vocabulary, give your child many opportunities to read new words.

Activity:

1. Identify several sight words your child is learning at school or several words that are repeatedly found in children's books such as *like, a, an, and, the, run, see, girl, can, boy, happy*, etc.

2. Give your child a page of a newspaper or magazine. Ask him or her to circle the two words he or she has selected every time he or she sees them. On other occasions repeat the activities with other words.

GA1509

Make It Purposeful

<table>
<tr><td>At-Home Objective:</td><td>Make reading meaningful by leaving important messages for your child.</td></tr>
<tr><td>Activity:</td><td>Write your child notes during the day. Instead of giving an instruction orally, hand your child a card, such as "It's time for dinner." "Do you want to play a game?" The more important the contents to the child the better.

These notes will get you started.</td></tr>
</table>

Love Notes

At-Home Objective: Motivate your child to read by making reading meaningful.

Activity: Put a sweet note in your child's lunch box or under his or her pillow. When you leave town for a few days, leave numbered notes, one for each day you are gone.

Use the page below for your first note.

A Note for You!

50

GA1509

Reading Time

At-Home Objective: Make the most of reading time with these simple steps. Your child will build an understanding of the reading process and a love for reading. If these steps are followed every time you read to your child, he or she is likely to pick up many reading skills by him- or herself.

Activity:

1. Before beginning to read a book, read the title. Ask "What do you think this book might be about? Let's read to find out."

2. As you read to your child, run your hand along the words as you say each one. Always move your hand from left to right.

3. Make it fun. Be very expressive when you read. Use different voices for different characters.

4. Talk about the pictures in the book. Every conversation encourages your child to use the meaningful cues available to the reader.

5. Occasionally before turning the page, ask your child, "What do you think might happen next?"

6. After reading a book, ask your child if he or she liked it and why.

J. Armbrust 93

MOTHER GOOSE

GA1509

Buzz. . . What's the Word?

At-Home Objective: Use this activity to teach and reinforce your child's spelling word list.

Activity: Call out spelling words that your child needs to know, and have your very own spelling bee.

52

GA1509

What Happened Next?

At-Home Objective: This activity will encourage your child to build prediction skills and to use information to form new conclusions.

Activity: When you are driving in the car, start a story. After awhile, pause and say, "Next, please." That's your child's cue to take over, repeat the important points of the story so far, and then add to the story.

Fill in the parts of a story your family tells. Be sure to let everyone have a turn.

53

GA1509

Next, Please

At-Home Objective: This activity teaches a child how to select a main idea and builds auditory memory skills.

Activity: At the dinner table, have each person share something that happened during the day. When everyone has finished, have the children identify one thing each person said. Fill in the people who sit around your dinner table. Label them by name.

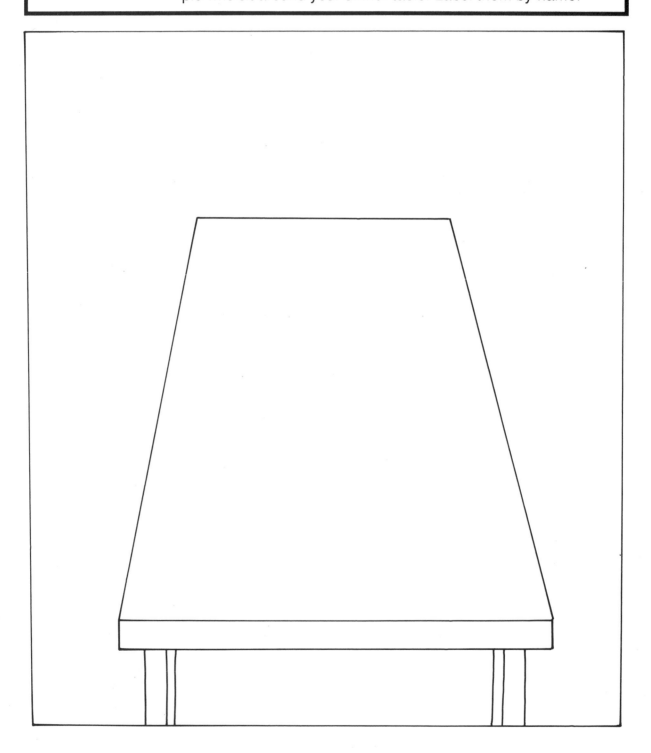

54

GA1509

TV Time

News for You

News Sense

The At-Home Gazette

Edition 1 _____   Date: _____

Find It in the News

At-Home Objective: Knowing how to use a table of contents is a very helpful skill.

Activity: Show your child the table of contents for the newspaper. Read the titles. Find out on what page each section of the paper begins. Using the table of contents, identify the page number for each item below; then find each item in the newspaper. Paste an article or picture from your favorite section of the newspaper on your front page below.

Table of Contents
Crossword Puzzle p. _____
Television Listing p. _____
Comics p. _____
Weather Report p. _____
Want Ads p. _____

GA1509

More News

At-Home Objective: These activities will help your child understand how a newspaper is put together and how to use the table of contents to find a particular section of the newspaper.

Activity: Show your child the front of the newspaper. Talk about the various items on the front page. Unfold the paper and look at each section. Write the names of the sections of the newspaper below.

59

GA1509

Opposites Unite

At-Home Objective: Reinforce your child's understanding of opposites with this activity.

Activity: Write the opposite of each word on the line. See how many you know.

GA1509

Alike and Different

Go-Togethers

At-Home Objective: With this activity your child will be able to categorize things that go together.

Activity: Some things simply seem to go together. Look at the pictures below. Which ones go together? Around your house there are also lots of things that go together. Below you'll find one half of a pair. Have your child name the item that goes with each one and draw a picture of it. Draw any other pair you think of in the blank boxes.

Give older children a series of index cards with one item on each card. Have your child match the cards to make sets of go-togethers.

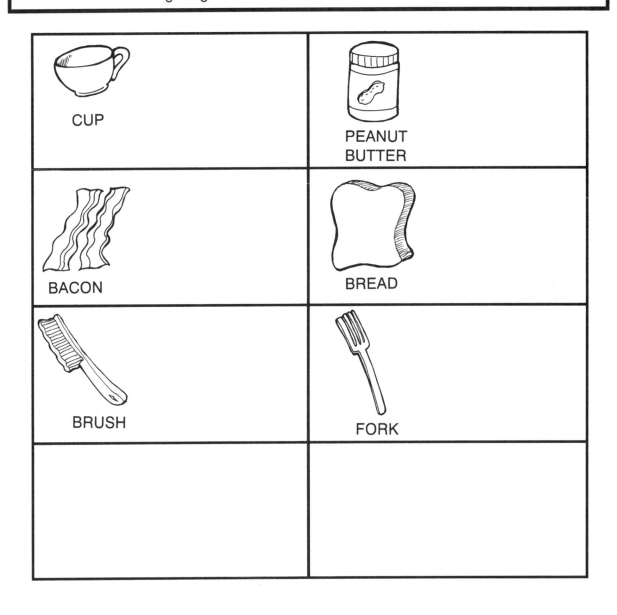

CUP	PEANUT BUTTER
BACON	BREAD
BRUSH	FORK

GA1509

Rhyme a Line

At-Home Objective: Expand your child's poetic skills by helping him or her rhyme lines.

Activity: Take turns making nonsense sentences about what you are doing and what you see around you. The child or parent supplies the first line. The other person completes the rhyme. Here are some silly examples to get you started.

There's some gooey jelly in the glass. . .

It's not easy to balance plates. . .

One, two, three chairs. . .

Have your child write his or her favorite silly poem on the lines below and illustrate it.

_____

_____

_____

_____

_____

GA1509

Rhyme Time

At-Home Objective: Teach your child to hear and supply rhyming words. Hearing and identifying the sounds at the end of words are important auditory discrimination skills.

Activity: When you are setting the table, washing the dishes, or driving in the car, have your child supply a rhyming word for an object you see. It is okay if it's not a real word as long as it rhymes. Find a word that rhymes with each picture.

PLATE

DISH

TABLE

SALT

GLASS

CHAIR

TREE

GA1509

Cook Time Rhymes

At-Home Objective: Learning to rhyme is a fun way to practice beginning sounds.

Activity: As you and your child work in the kitchen, play a rhyming game. Each time someone names a word associated with the kitchen, the other person must supply a word that rhymes with that word. For example, start with *cook*. Your child might say *book*. Then it is your child's turn. Nonsense words count!

Other easily rhymed words include *fork, floor, mat, can, box, pot, hot.*

GA1509

Snip Art

At-Home Objective: Teach your child how to identify the syllables in words.

Activity: Name the objects in the room. Have the older child write the words in very big letters on index cards, separating each word between syllables. Have your child snip each word between syllables. For a younger child or less able reader, write the word on the card, separating the syllables. Have the child snip at the syllable and repeat it.

GA1509

Puzzle Time

At-Home Objective: Learning to read the syllables in words is a helpful word recognition strategy.

Activity: Have your child cut out the puzzle words. Read each one, exaggerating the syllables. Cut the words between syllables. Mix the syllables up and have him or her put the snipped syllables together to make real words.

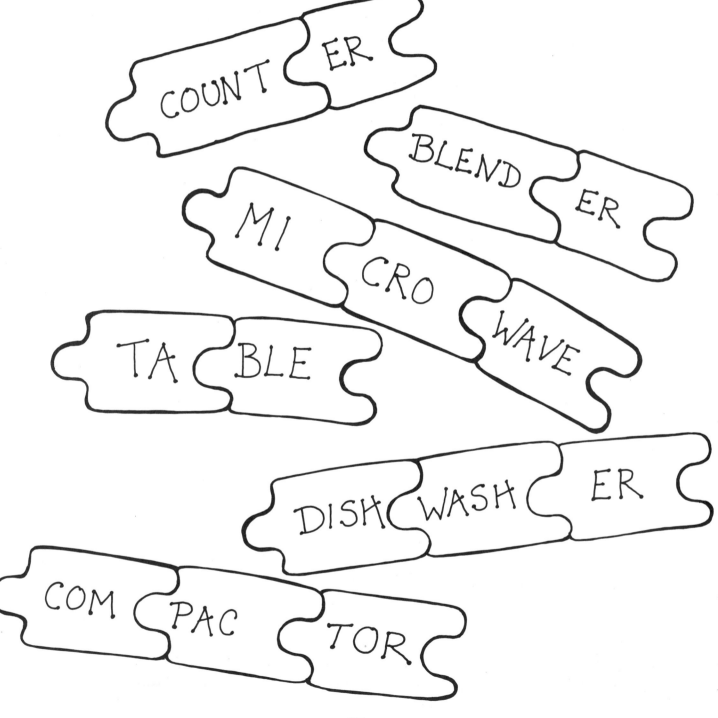

GA1509

Syllable Clap

At-Home Objective: Help your child learn how to identify the names of objects and to divide words into syllables.

Activity: While you are working in any room of the house, have your child go around the room naming various items in the room. Each time he or she names something, have him or her exaggerate the syllables, clap the number of syllables, and give you the number.

Write the name of each object you find in the house below. Draw a line between the syllables.

GA1509

A Whale of a Story

Finish the Story

You can have so much fun writing stories. You can go anywhere – anytime; just use your mind and have a great time. Use your imagination and have fun with writing!

Be creative, finish each sentence and help make the story complete.

My sister went to camp and _____

_____

_____

She wrote me a letter and told me that_____

_____

_____

When she finally came home I _____

_____

_____

None of us could believe that she _____

_____

_____

One day I want to go to camp but_____

_____

_____

I can't wait until next summer because_____

_____

_____

The Apple of My Eye

At-Home Objective: Use this activity as a creative writing exercise.

Activity: Choose someone that you really like a lot and write a story about why he or she is special.

71

GA1509

Loose Tooth

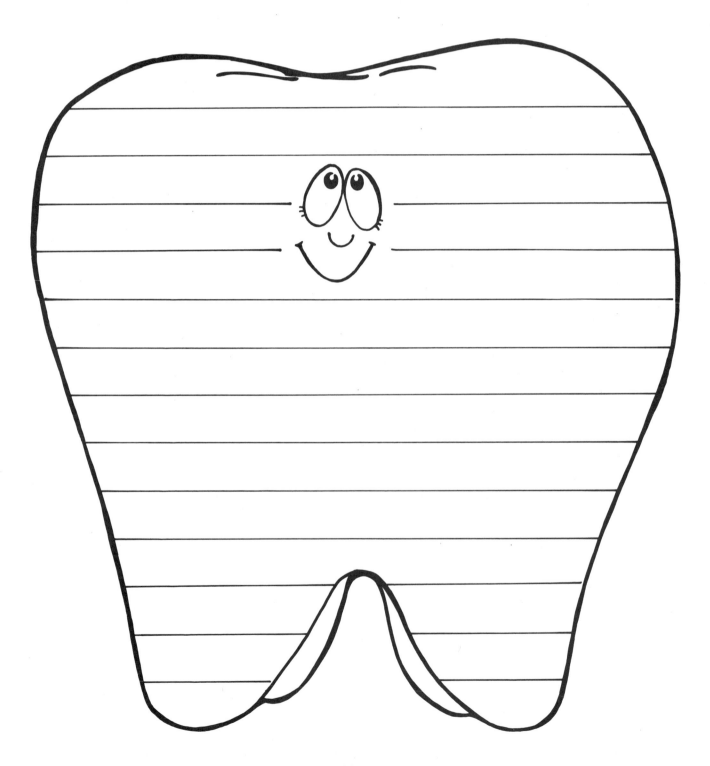

GA1509

Award an Award!

At-Home Objective: Use this activity to encourage creative writing.

Activity: Surprise a family member with a special award. Write what makes this person special on it.

GA1509

Book This Date!

At-Home Objective: Use this creative writing activity to help your child understand a particular book and author's style.

Activity: Honor your favorite author by planning a special birthday party. Design an invitation that represents the book and the author's style.

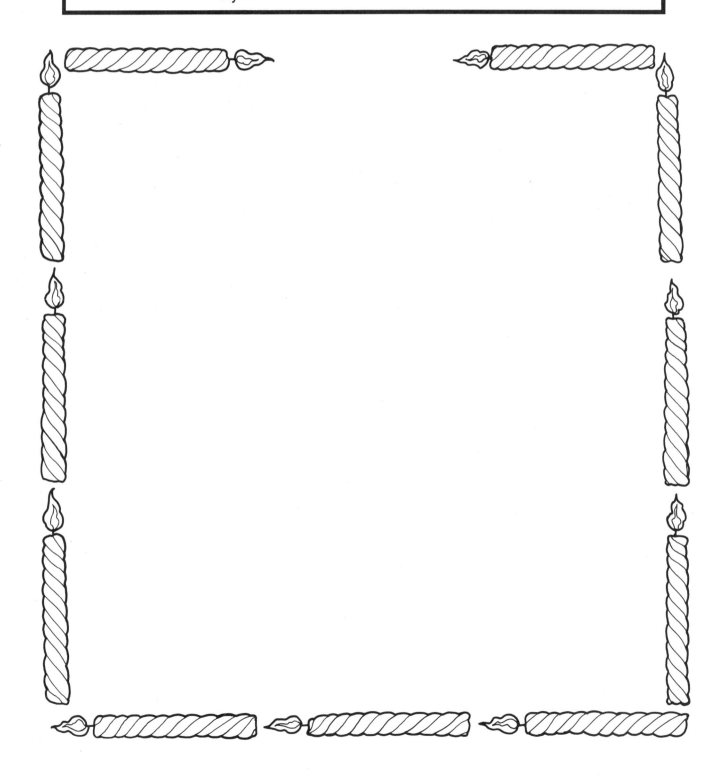

74

GA1509

Around and Around We Go!

At-Home Objective: Use this creative writing activity to encourage your child's writing skills.

Activity: Write a story starting in the center of this circle, and keep turning your paper around and around until you fill up the entire circle. Cut it out when you are finished.

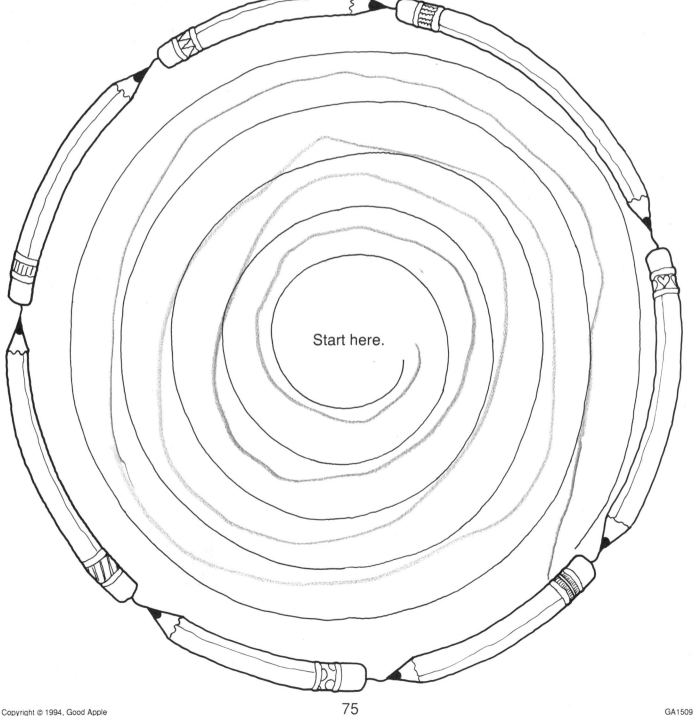

Start here.

GA1509

Make Your Own Comic

At-Home Objective: Encourage a creative writing activity with this exercise.

Activity: You are a cartoonist. Create a character and draw two comic strips starring your creation.

GA1509

All About Me

At-Home Objective:	Use this creative writing activity to encourage a positive self-concept.
Activity:	Draw a self-portrait, and then write something special that you like about yourself.

GA1509

Bumper Up

At-Home Objective: Use this creative writing activity to help a good cause.

Activity: Design a bumper sticker to show your support or concern about any topic.

78

Thank You from the Bottom of My Heart

At-Home Objective: Encourage your child's writing skills with this activity.

Activity: Write a thank-you letter to someone who has done a good deed for you or who has been thoughtful.

79

GA1509

Give Me a Hand

At-Home Objective: Use this activity to work on good handwriting habits.

Activity: Find a poem or rhyme that you really like, and rewrite it on this page to show off your excellent handwriting skills.

80

Make a Diary

Activity:

All those old odds and ends of stationery can have a new use. Combine old stationery and other colored paper into a book. Have your child cut all the pages the same size. Use a hole punch to cut three holes in the same place on the left-hand side of each page. Bind the book by threading yarn through the holes.

Teach your child how to write the date (month, day, year) at the top of a page.

Encourage your child to keep the diary each day by writing anything he or she likes. Assure him or her that spelling isn't important.

Social Studies

GA1509

The Family Rules

At-Home Objective: Use this activity to encourage your child's awareness of rules and what they mean.

Activity: When a group of people are together in a community, they need rules. Rules help a family get along too. Can you list the rules your family has in your house?

1. _____

_____

2. _____

_____

3. _____

_____

4. _____

_____

5. _____

_____

6. _____

_____

7. _____

_____

GA1509

Community Helpers

Activity: There are many community helpers who make our world a better place to live. Draw a line to match the correct object with the community helper it belongs to, and color each object when you finish.

POLICE OFFICER

TEACHER

NURSE

FIRE FIGHTER

DENTIST

Share and Share Alike!

At-Home Objective: Use this activity to talk with your child about the services and places that make your neighborhood and community a better place.

Activity: Put a circle around each of the places or things that you can find in your community that helps you or your family.

85

GA1509

My Neighborhood

At-Home Objective:	Use this activity to encourage your child's awareness of your neighborhood and surroundings.
Activity:	When families live near one another, this is called a neighborhood. Draw a picture of your favorite things that make up your neighborhood.

COURT · NEIGHBOR'S SWIMMING POOL · BEAUTIFUL FLOWERS · BEAUTIFUL LAWNS · THE ZOO · THE SCHOOLS · CHRISTMAS · LIGHTS · TRICK OR TREATING · CHURCH · ICE SKATING · BOWLING · ROLLER SKATING · GOOD FRIENDS · FRIENDS · TREES · RIDING BIKES · PLAYING IN THE PARK · THE BASKETBALL

GA1509

Right Next Door!

GA1509

My Family

_____

_____

The Farmer in the Dell

At-Home Objective: This activity takes you outside. Your child will learn a lot more about farming when he or she plants his or her own vegetables.

Activity: Select one vegetable for your child to grow. Help him or her pick a well-lit spot in the yard for a garden. Read the instructions on the seed package together and take care of the plant daily.

Keep a record of the day when you plant the seed, when it pops through the soil, and when you pick the first vegetable. How long did it take to grow the vegetable?

Plant showing on _____

Planted seed on _____

First harvest on _____

GA1509

Farmyard Blues

At-Home Objective: There are many ways of life. Some people live in the city; others live in a rural area. Help your child understand the differences between city life and rural life.

Activity: Complete the pictures of a farmhouse and city house.

What kinds of things would you find in the city?
What kinds of things would you find in the country?

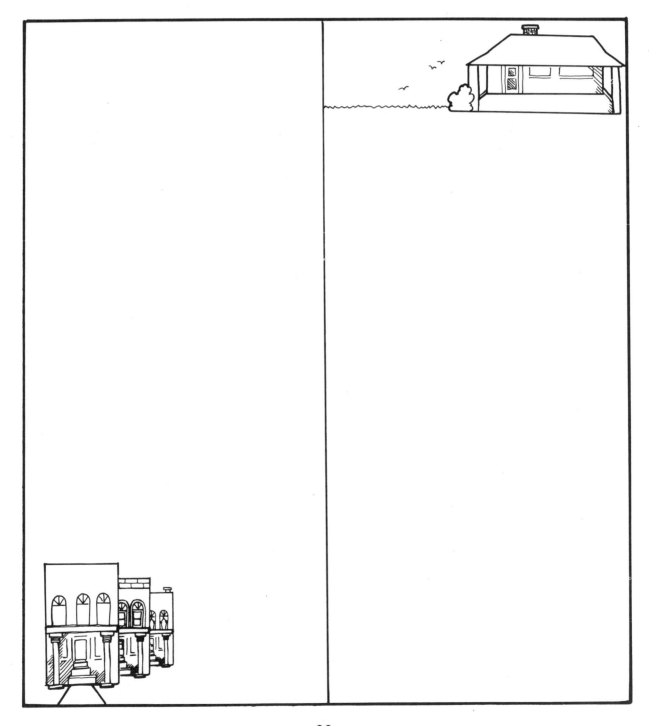

90

GA1509

Population

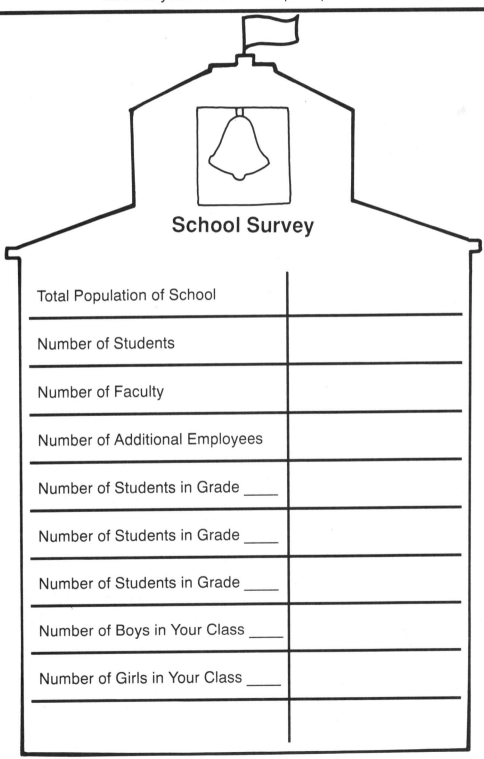

School Survey

Total Population of School	
Number of Students	
Number of Faculty	
Number of Additional Employees	
Number of Students in Grade ____	
Number of Students in Grade ____	
Number of Students in Grade ____	
Number of Boys in Your Class ____	
Number of Girls in Your Class ____	

GA1509

Who Are Your Neighbors?

At-Home Objective: We have all kinds of neighbors--neighbors on our street, neighboring states and neighboring countries. Here's a way to teach that concept.

Activity: Take a walk on your streets. Point out the homes on both sides of yours. Who are your neighbors? Sitting at the dinner table, ask your child who his or her neighbors are. Look at the map below. Find your state (province). Who are your neighbors? Color the neighbor on the north blue, the neighbor on the south red, the neighbor on the east yellow, and the neighbor on the west green.

GA1509

At Home Sweet Home

The Constitution

THE CONSTITUTION

_____

_____

_____

_____

_____

_____

_____

_____

_____

_____

_____

_____

GA1509

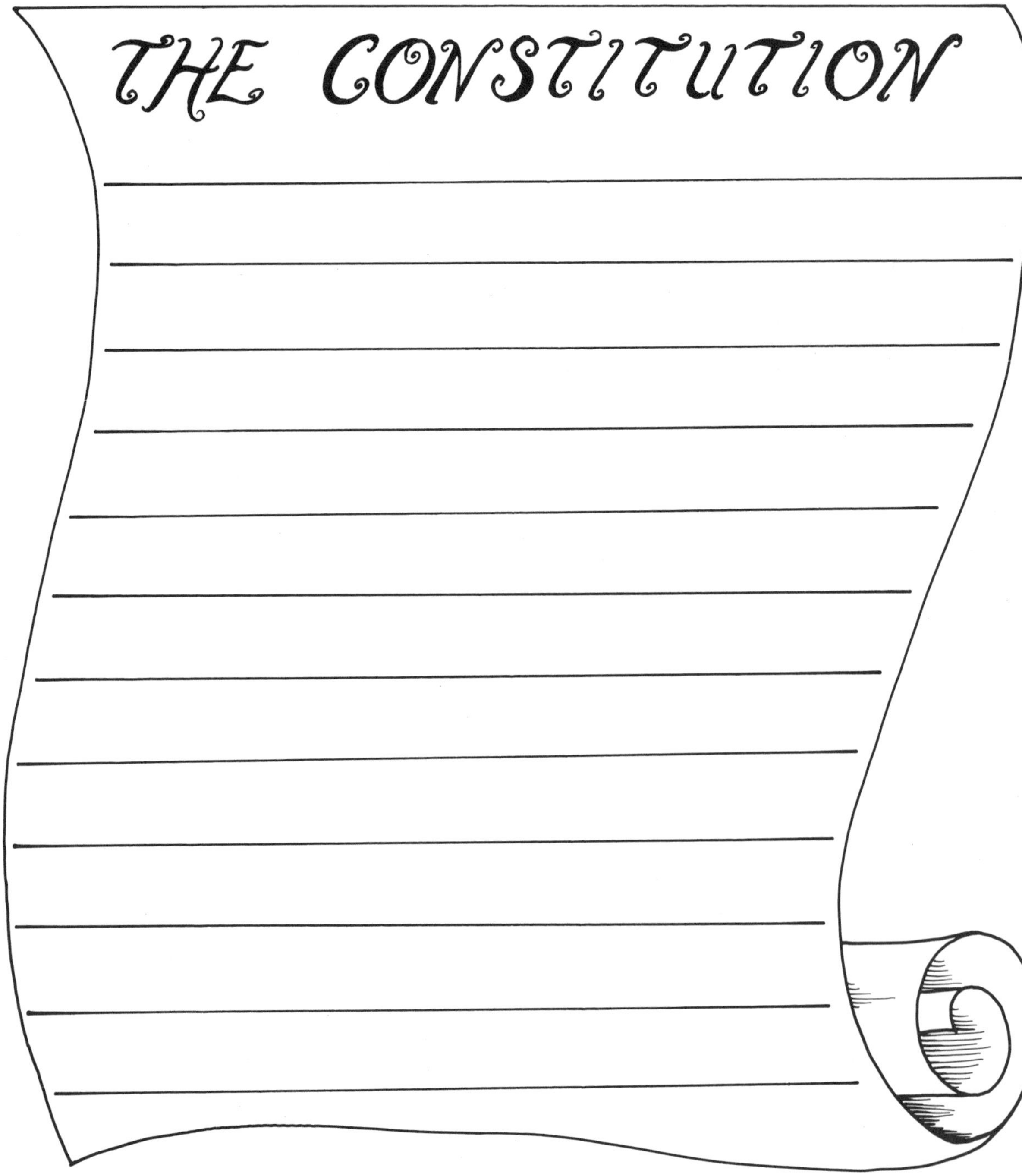

Be a Good Citizen

At-Home Objective: Each of us has a responsibility as a citizen of the country in which we live to help improve the country and the lives of its people. Help your child recognize his or her responsibility by modeling good citizenship.

Activity: Talk about the kinds of things citizens should do. When you go to the park, take a trash bag to collect extra trash you find. When you go to vote, take your child with you. Explain the procedures and what the election is about. Have your child make an ad to remind people to be good citizens.

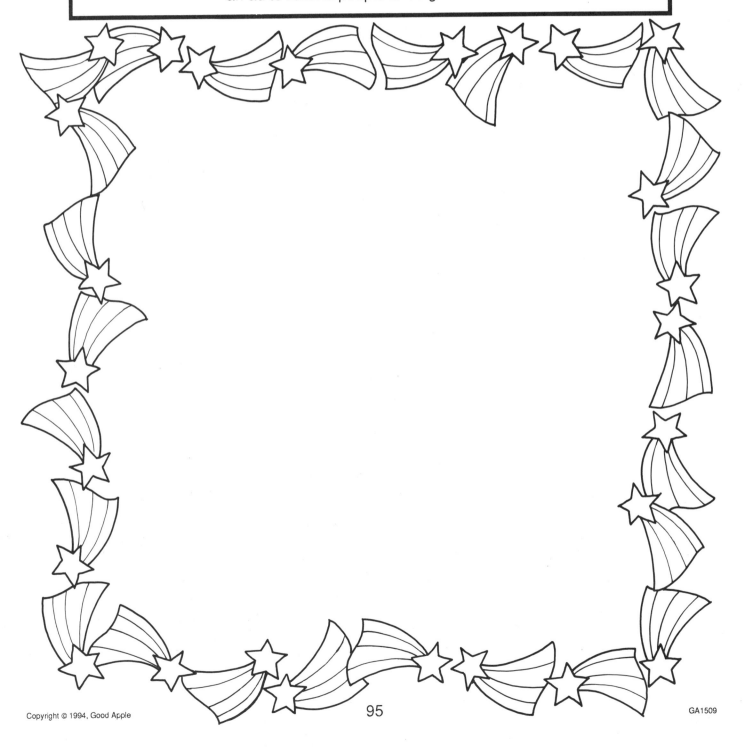

GA1509

Who Are the People in Your Government?

At-Home Objective: Understanding the roles and responsibilities of being a good citizen should begin very early. Take every opportunity to model qualities of good citizenship.

Activity: Visit the capitol building of your state (province) or your local city hall. Explain to your child what the jobs of your local leaders are. Have your child fill in the names and titles of your local leaders. On the flag below, write the names of your government officials.

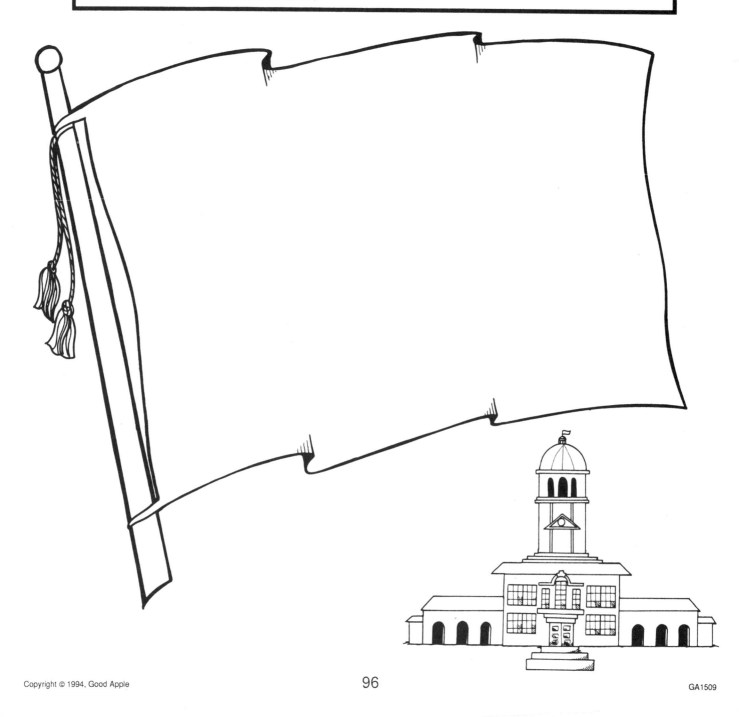

96

GA1509

Going Up

At-Home Objective: Prices change for many reasons. Use this shopping list to teach your child a lesson in economy.

Activity: Take this shopping list to the store every week for two months, or track the prices in the grocery pages. How much do the prices change? Do the weather, the time of year, or other reasons seem to change the prices?

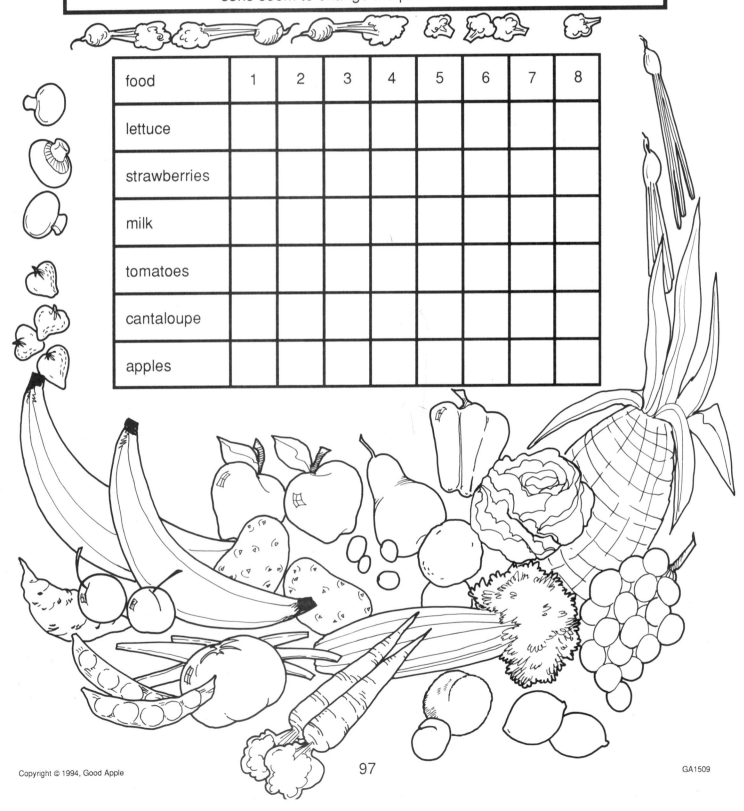

food	1	2	3	4	5	6	7	8
lettuce								
strawberries								
milk								
tomatoes								
cantaloupe								
apples								

97

GA1509

It's the Law

At-Home Objective: Use this opportunity to get your child to think about the kinds of laws that should be made.

Activity: Every year the government enacts new laws. One example is the seat belt law. Ask your child what he or she thinks about this law. Have your child write five reasons why children should wear helmets when they ride bikes or why school buses should have seat belts. Send the list to your local government officials.

Dear _____,

I believe we need a law to

_____

_____

Here are my reasons why.

1. _____

2. _____

3. _____

4. _____

5. _____

Thank you for your time.

Sincerely,

_____

GA1509

It's History

At-Home Objective: You know many facts about history that your child would enjoy knowing. Let him or her interview you for this activity.

Activity: Your parents have lived much longer than you. In fact much of their "history" is now in your history book. You'll be surprised by what you will learn by asking.

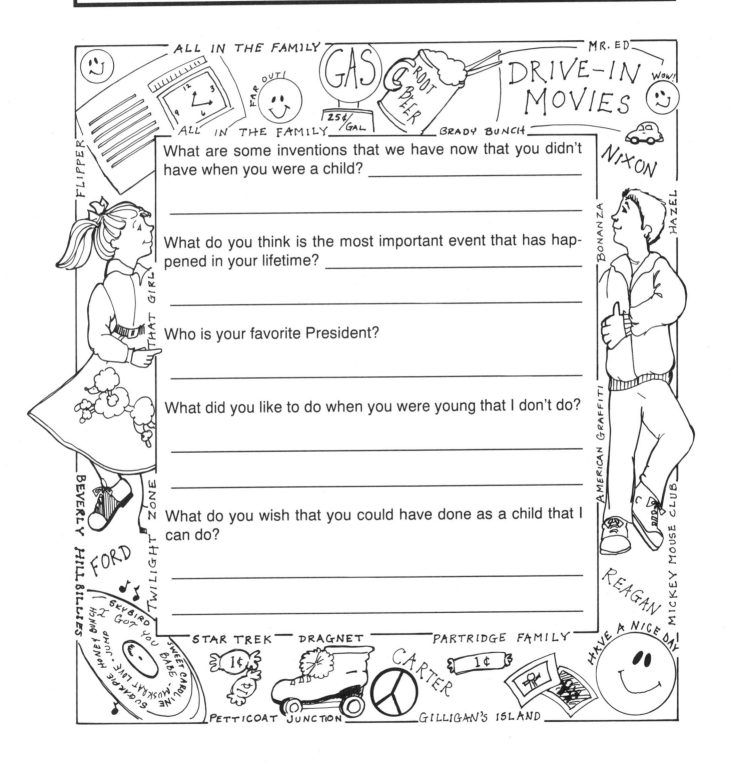

What are some inventions that we have now that you didn't have when you were a child? _____

_____

What do you think is the most important event that has happened in your lifetime? _____

_____

Who is your favorite President?

_____

What did you like to do when you were young that I don't do?

_____

_____

What do you wish that you could have done as a child that I can do?

_____

_____

GA1509

It's a Grand, Old Flag

At-Home Objective:	What does your child know about his or her country's flag? Use this activity to teach about this symbol.
Activity:	Have your child complete the flag by drawing in the appropriate parts, and coloring the entire flag.

GA1509

Make a Family Tree

At-Home Objective: Teach your child that history is a living thing by discussing your family's ancestry.

Activity: Using the tree below, fill in your family tree together. If you can find photographs of the people, glue the tree to poster board and add pictures for each member.

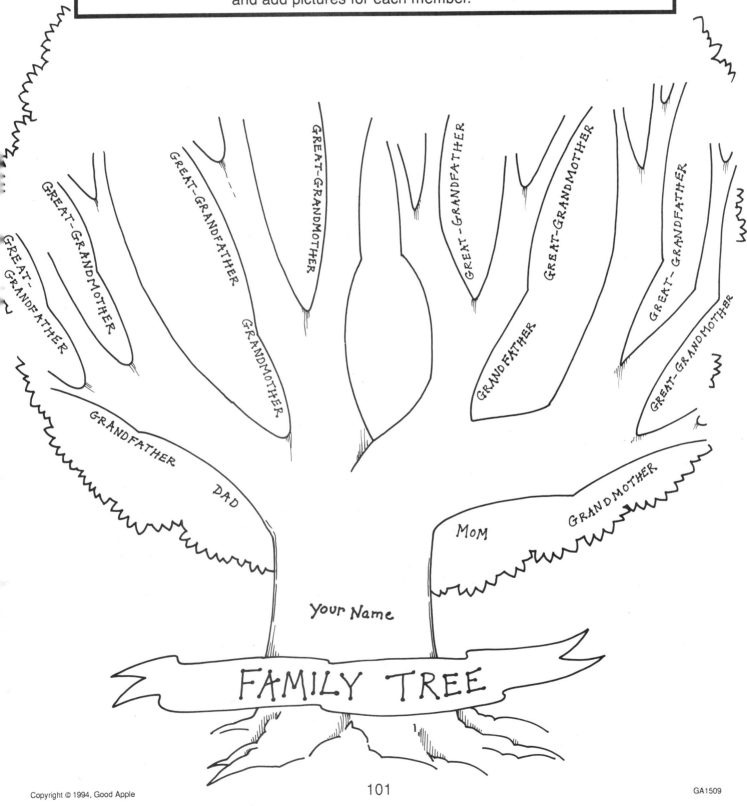

GA1509

Real-Life Studies

At-Home Objective:	Make history a living thing by sharing memories with your child.
Activity:	When the grandparents or an older relative comes to visit, make it an ongoing project to have your child interview the relative. Copy the interview form as many times as needed. Compile the interviews in a scrapbook. Have your child make a cover for the project.

Interview

Name: ______________________________

Date of Birth: ______________________________

Place of Birth: ______________________________

Favorite Memory of Childhood: ______________________________

____

____

What's most different about life now as compared with when you grew up?

____

____

____

What event in history that occurred during your life do you think was most important?

____

____

____

Transportation

At-Home Objective: People didn't always drive in cars. Help your child understand the history of transportation.

Activity: How many ways can you think of to get from one place to another? List them in the space below. Draw pictures on another sheet of paper of all the kinds of transportation you can think of.

When and where might these kinds of transportation be used?

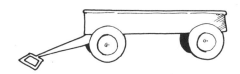

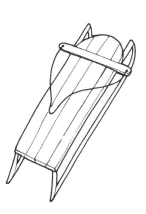

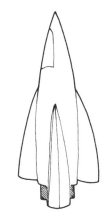

1. _____
2. _____
3. _____
4. _____
5. _____
6. _____
7. _____
8. _____
9. _____
10. _____

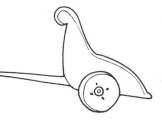

GA1509

Make a Time Line

GA1509

Connect the TV to the World

At-Home Objective:	Make the current events your child hears on the news and at the dinner table a part of your discussion. Bring them to life by involving your child in understanding them.
Activity:	Post a world map next to the television. Whenever a location in the world is mentioned, help your child find it on the map. Keep a record of the places you find below. At the end of each week review the places you have found. Show your child how to use an almanac to locate information about a place. Even a simple dictionary provides valuable information. Write one fact about each place.

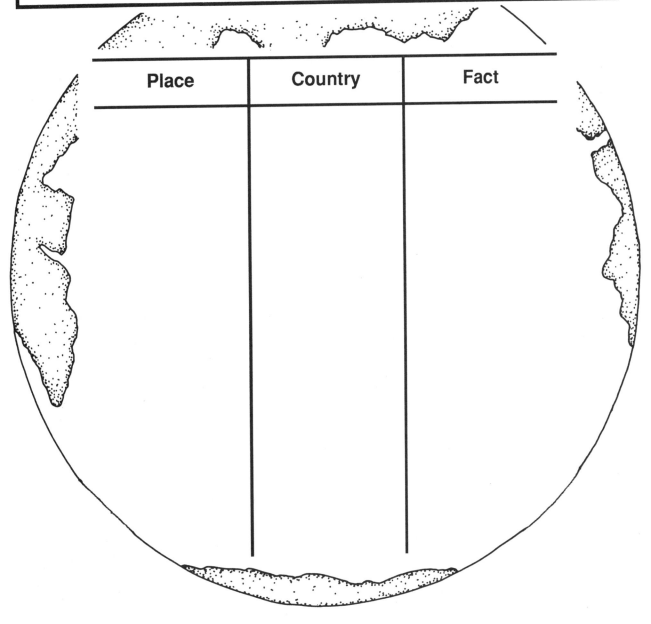

Place	Country	Fact

GA1509

Map It Out!

At-Home Objective: Use this activity to encourage your child to learn how to use a map.

Activity: Provide your child with a map of any kind. Pick two cities and have your child draw a line that connects the destinations. See how many cities and countries you have to go through to get from one place to the other. What kind of transportation will you need? Have your child list some of the highlights of your trip and the names of the places you visit along the way.

GA1509

Make a Word Search

At-Home Objective:	Use this activity to encourage your child to expand his or her awareness of the cities in the United States or Canada.
Activity:	Show how "worldly" your vocabulary is. List a variety of cities that you have either visited or would like to visit one day. Fill the empty squares in with assorted alphabet letters and give a friend this word search to try. Be sure to list the cities that you have hidden for your friend to find.

Can you find these cities?

Where Are You?

At-Home Objective: Use this activity to encourage an awareness of the states or provinces that make up your country.

Activity: Look through the newspaper and cut out the names of as many different states (provinces) as you can find, and glue them on this map in the correct locations. Refer to a map or a globe for extra help.

Moving Right Along

At-Home Objective: One way to get an understanding of your country is to travel it. Where has your child been?

Activity: Color in all the areas you have visited on the map. Find one place you would like to go and tell your parent (guardian) about it. Where would you find these other famous places?

St. Louis

Washington, D.C.

GA1509

What's in a Name?

At-Home Objective: Lots of people have nicknames. You or your child might even have one. Your child can learn something new about your state when you discuss its nickname.

Activity: Many states have nicknames. Use the encyclopedia to match these states with their nicknames:

Peach State	Nevada
Grand Canyon State	Illinois
First State	Delaware
Bluegrass State	Hawaii
Land of Lincoln	New York
Silver State	Texas
Empire State	Kentucky
Lone Star State	Georgia
Aloha State	Arizona

What is your state's nickname?

Draw the license plate for your state with a symbol for it.

110

GA1509

Which Is Bigger?

At-Home Objective: One of the hardest concepts for a young child to learn is the difference between a city, a state, and a country. Help your child learn this.

Activity: Look at a map of your state or province. Draw a facsimile of your state or province. Place a dot on the map to represent your city. Ask your child which is bigger, the city or the state, the state or the country, etc.

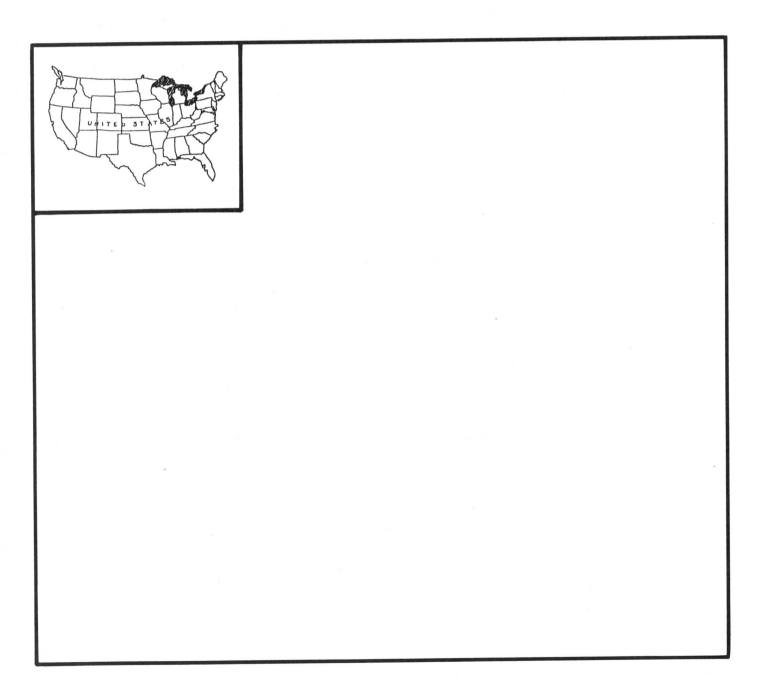

111

GA1509

News Around the World

At-Home Objective:	Use this activity to teach your child how to identify and locate states or provinces on the map.
Activity:	After you've read the front section of the newspaper, hand it to your child. Challenge him or her to find as many states' (provinces') names on the first ______ pages as possible. Show him or her how to circle the name of each with a marker. Write the name of each city, state, or province your child finds below.

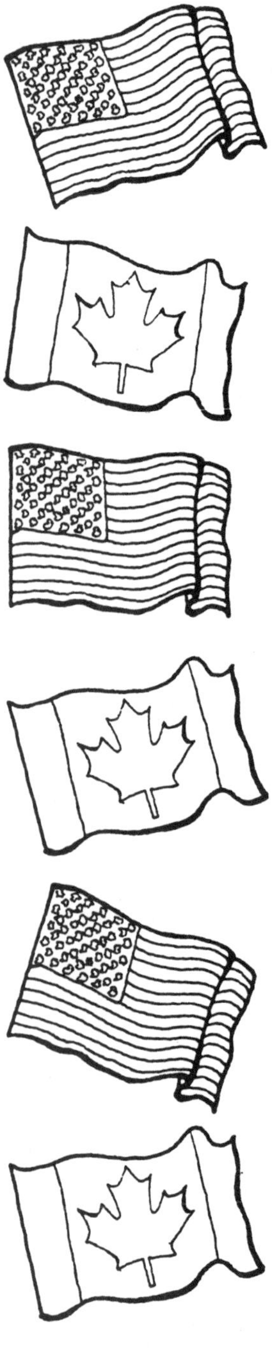

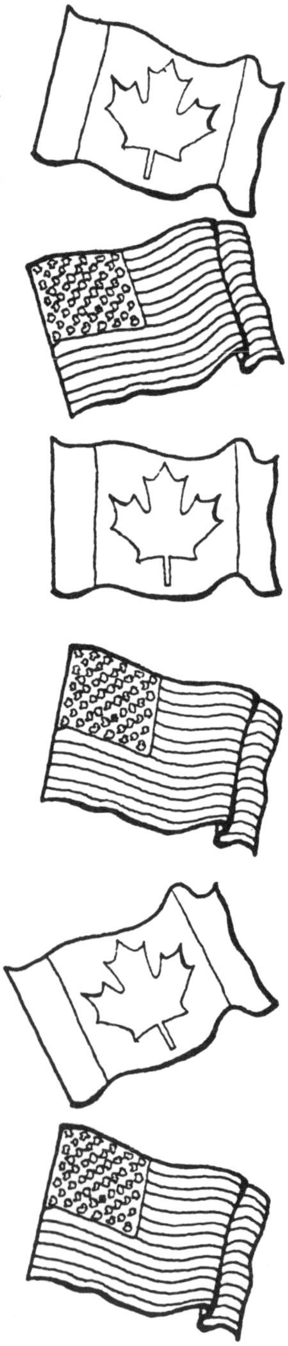

North, East, South, and West

GA1509

Point Me in the Right Direction

At-Home Objective: Reinforce your child's knowledge of direction.

Activity:

1. Remind your child of the directions north, east, south, west. Identify which way is N, S, E, W in your home. Which side of the house faces west, east, north, south? Walk into each room of the house and have your child identify the directions.

2. Have your child follow these directions and see which way he or she ends up facing.

    Take two steps to the east.
    Take one big jump north.
    Face south.
    Take two steps south.
    Which way are you facing?

Have your child draw or write the directions he or she is going to give you. Which way did you end up facing?

114

GA1509

Make a Map

At-Home Objective: Use this activity to help your child learn about directions and distance.

Activity: Draw a map of the way you go to school each morning.

GA1509

Pack It Up!

At-Home Objective: Use this activity to encourage your child's interest in another country.

Activity: Pretend that you are going on a trip to another country. Read all about it or interview someone who has been there, and then pack up everything you might need to take with you. Draw a picture of the things you'll need in your suitcase. What kind of clothes should you take?

116

GA1509

Moving On!

At-Home Objective: Use this activity to encourage your child's awareness of the different kinds of transportation throughout the world.

Activity: People throughout the world use different kinds of transportation to get from one place to another. Draw as many kinds of transportation as you can think of and color them in.

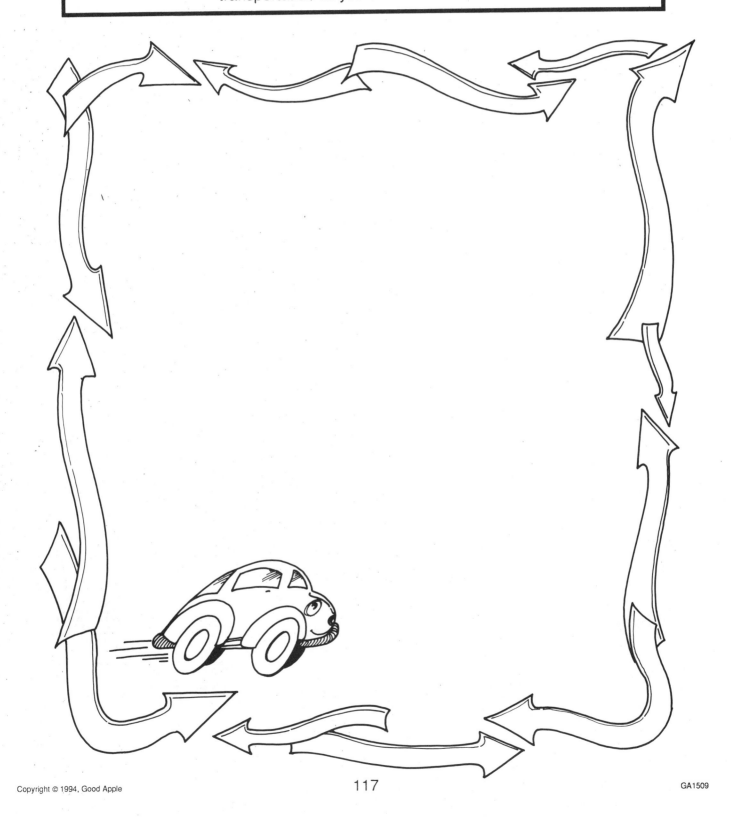

117

GA1509

All About Japan

At-Home Objective: Use this activity to learn about another country.

Activity: Find out everything you can about China and Japan, and list all the new vocabulary words that you learned on this page.

Words I Learned About China and Japan

118

GA1509

Around the World in Eighty Days!

At-Home Objective: Use this activity to stimulate your child's interest in learning about faraway places.

Activity: Pretend you are going to travel all around the world. Look at a globe and decide what path you'll take and which countries you'll travel through to go all the way around the world. List the countries you travel through on this page.

GA1509

Talk! Talk! Talk!

At-Home Objective: Use this activity to teach your child about different cultures and their languages.

Activity: Interview a variety of people and find out about as many different languages as you can. List each language on this page and see how long you can make your list.

120

Dress Up!

At-Home Objective: Use this activity to encourage your child to learn about how clothing differs in each culture.

Activity: Find out how a different culture dresses and dress these characters correctly.

GA1509

Homeward Bound!

At-Home Objective: Use this activity to encourage your child to learn about another country.

Activity: You have just visited another country. Learn all about it, and then pack your suitcase filled with things that you want to take home from there. Fill your suitcase with pictures of the objects.

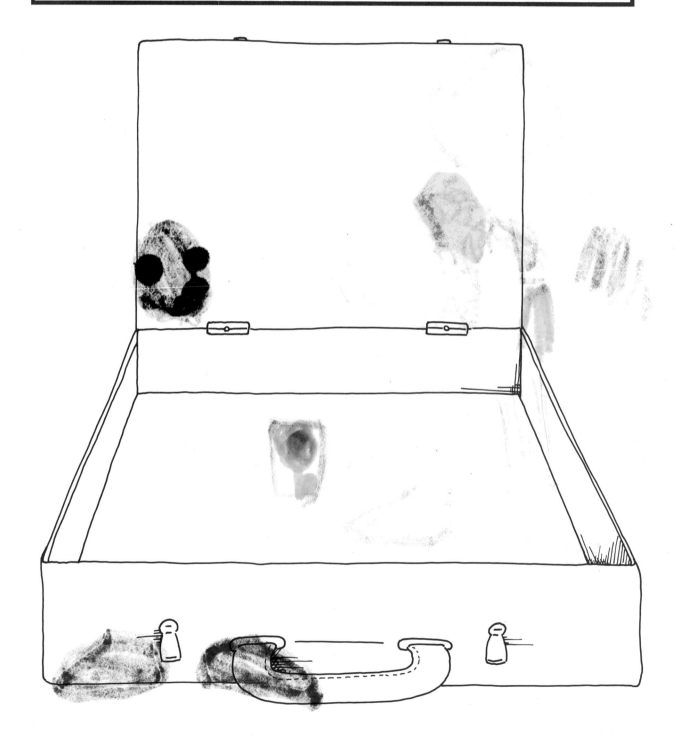

GA1509

Questions and Answers

GA1509

Where on Earth?

At-Home Objective: Use this activity to encourage your child's awareness of the world around him or her.

Activity: On another piece of paper, keep a list for one week of all the return addresses on the mail that your family receives. Every time you find a city and state (province) record it on the correct place on the map.

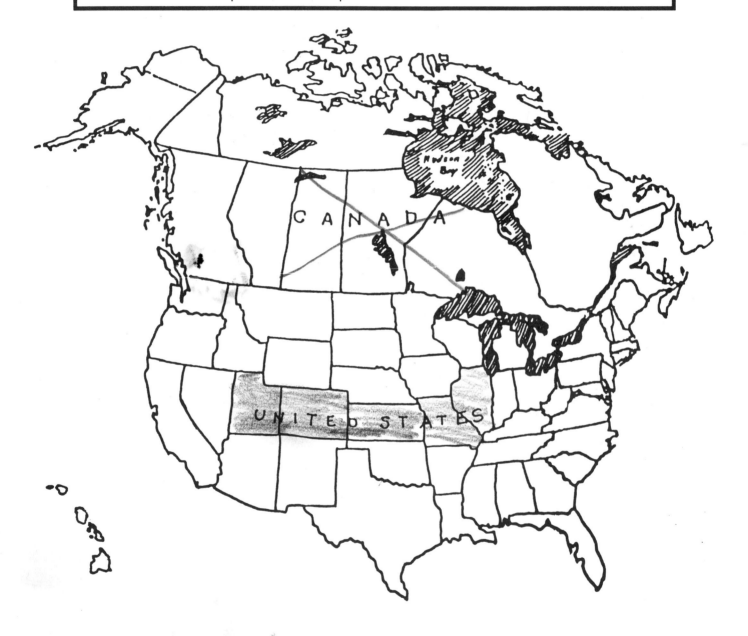

GA1509

Telephone Fun

At-Home Objective: The telephone book provides many opportunities for learning. Help your child understand the various kinds of jobs people have by looking in the Yellow Pages.

Activity: Flip through the Yellow Pages. List ten kinds of jobs you find. Try to find information about these jobs: plumber, baker, electrician.

Create your own ad for one of the occupations you find.

GA1509

Responsibility

At-Home Objective: Everyone has jobs. Members of a family help take care of one another. One of the ways we do this is with family jobs or chores.

Activity:

1. Talk about what it means to be a member of the family. Talk about the kinds of jobs that must be done. Being a family member means that everyone has a responsibility.

2. Make a job chart. Talk about the kinds of jobs members of the family might have. With a magic marker, divide a paper plate into various sectors. Trace an arrow onto a piece of construction paper and attach it to the plate with a brad. Each week have your child point the arrow to the job he or she selects for that week. If there are more children in the family, spin the arrow to select weekly chores. Mark the chores on the chart.

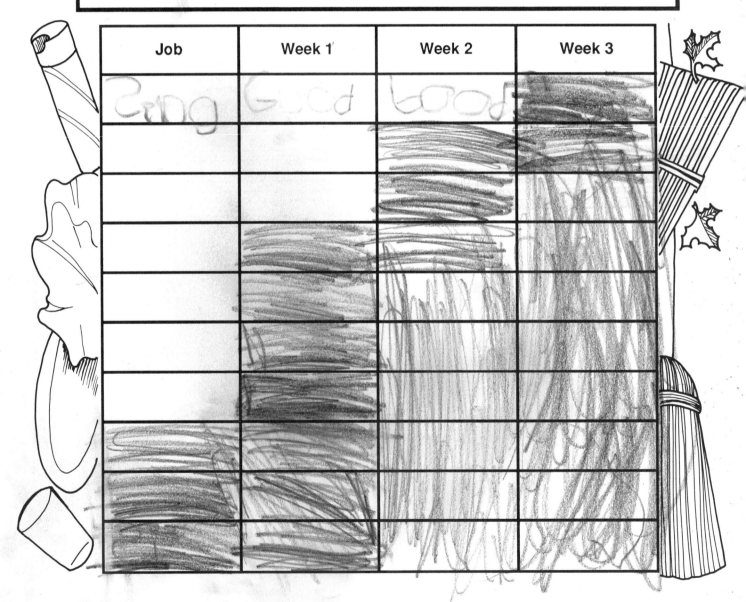

Job	Week 1	Week 2	Week 3

Learn All About It!

At-Home Objective: Use this activity to teach your child about totem poles and what they stand for.

Activity: Learn all about totem poles, and then design your own on this page. Totem poles actually represent information about a family. See what else you can find out about them, and then draw a totem pole that represents your family.

127

Hello, World

At-Home Objective: People may look and dress differently, but we are more alike than different. Use this activity to improve your child's critical thinking skills.

Activity: Every language has a word for *hello* and *good-bye*. Guess where each of these children is from. Make a list of ways people are alike.

Here are ways that people are alike.

1. SHALOM
2. ARRIVED ERCI
3. SAYONARA
4. BONJOUR
5. SAYONARA
6. _____
7. _____

128

Shopping Around the World

At-Home Objective:	The grocery store is a vast treasure of tasty experiences from around the world. Introduce your child to new foods and new countries around the world.
Activity:	Identify items in the grocery store that come from other countries. Often the pictures on the package as well as the information on the label will identify the country an item is from.
	As you walk through the grocery store, look for these items and identify what country they come from. Look for other items from other countries.

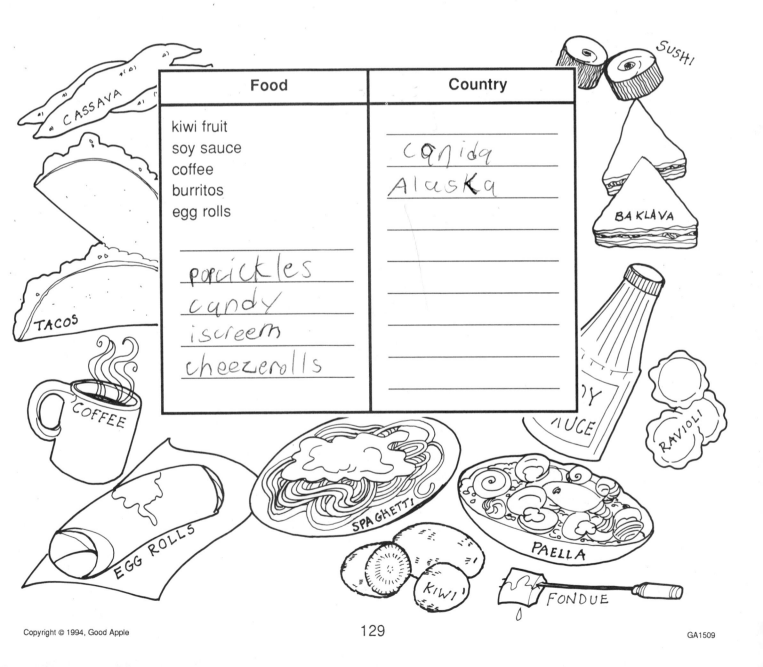

Food	Country
kiwi fruit	canida
soy sauce	Alaska
coffee	
burritos	
egg rolls	
porcickles	
candy	
iscreem	
cheezerolls	

CASSAVA

SUSHI

BAKLAVA

TACOS

COFFEE

EGG ROLLS

SPAGHETTI

SOY SAUCE

RAVIOLI

PAELLA

KIWI

FONDUE

GA1509

Travel Abroad at Home

At-Home Objective: Teach your child about other cultures.

Activity:

1. Make dinners adventuresome and educational. Introduce your child to a foreign country through the food you eat. When you have pizza, identify Italy on the map and the language the people speak. If you have clothes from the country or other artifacts, use them to make the event even more special.

2. Have your child select a country he or she would like to visit. Look it up in the encyclopedia. Visit an ethnic shop in your city. Look at artwork by artists from the country at the local museum. Send a letter to the official consulate of the country in Washington, D.C., or your community if there is one. Request information about the country.

GA1509

Here Is My Career

At-Home Objective: Use this activity to encourage your child to learn all about a specific career that interests him or her.

Activity: Choose one career and investigate it. Try to observe a person engaged in this career, and write a want ad and job description that tells exactly what skills are necessary for the career.

The career I picked is _____

GA1509

Day by Day

At-Home Objective: Use this activity to encourage your child to learn about a variety of careers.

Activity: List all the careers that help you during an entire day. For example, the mail carrier brings your mail. See how long you can make your list.

132

Household Jobs

At-Home Objective: Use this activity to encourage your child's awareness of the importance of jobs.

Activity: Jobs are very important to our community and our life. Think about the jobs you do at home, and write a story about how you help at home.

GA1509

When I Grow Up!

At-Home Objective: Use this activity to encourage your child to think about a career that interests him or her.

Activity: Draw a picture of yourself doing what you'd like to do when you grow up. Write the name of the career you have chosen.

When I grow up I want to be a _____.

GA1509

Careers in the News

READ ALL ABOUT IT!

135

My Career Dictionary

JOCKEY · TENNIS PRO. · TENNIS PRO · TV STAR · ASTRONAUT · ARCHAEOLOGIST · FARMER · MUSICIAN · VETERINARIAN · WRITER · ARTIST · MOM · COMPUTER WHIZ · SCIENTIST · RADIO DISC JOCKEY · CHIEF · NURSE · LAWYER · DOCTOR · TRUCK DRIVER · FIRE FIGHTER · FLORIST · ACTOR · NURSE · LIBRARIAN · DOG TRAINER · CHILDCARE · DAD · BANKER · PRESIDENT

1. last dog I miss
2. MY dog
3. He the I K
4. I'm training the
5. letter KK and dog

6.
7.
8.
9.
10.

All over the World Word Search

Words to Look For

people
world
airplane
flag
bus ✓
earth
city
laws
mail
ocean ✓

```
        R  S  P  A  E  T  W  E
     E  D  T  E  N  F  M  D  U  Y
  M  O  D  O  O  B  C  A  I  J  R  C
V  E  W  R  H  P  D  M  I  X  L  S  J  Z
J  G  N  V  K  V  L  G  D  L  Q  F  L  A  G  Y
P  L  W  K  F  J  E  U  G  L  T  Z  H  S  H  B
F  A  E  T  X  M  V  B  I  C  A  S  C  A  R  G
I  W  D  Z  F  O  C  E  A  N  G  Y  K  X  H  W
P  S  L  W  A  U  M  A  B  L  W  O  R  L  D  K
M  N  Q  O  I  K  R  C  M  B  J  S  L  R  N  O
Q  C  G  J  R  D  V  Y  E  C  U  X  F  K  T  I
L  I  Y  E  P  P  O  L  U  I  W  H  S  P  Z  X
   X  H  P  L  R  A  U  X  T  T  M  V  Y  Z
      N  Q  A  V  E  B  D  Y  C  P  O  Z
         W  N  Z  R  M  F  A  N  Z  B
            E  A  Y  E  A  R  T  H
                  B  U  S
```

List the words in alphabetical order.

1. People

2. World

3. _____

4. _____

5. bus

6. _____

7. _____

8. _____

9. _____

10. ocean

Don't Be Late . . . Communicate!

At-Home Objective:	Use this activity to teach your child about the various means of communication.
Activity:	Think of all the ways you communicate or the world communicates with you. Draw a picture of each object or example of communication. Example: telephone

Focus on Feelings

At-Home Objective: Use this activity to encourage your child to discuss needs and wants.

Activity: Each individual in a community has needs and wants. A need is something you must have to live, while a want is something you might like to have but do not need. List or draw a picture of your needs and wants to show that you understand the difference.

I Need:

I Want:

GA1509

Extra! Extra!
Read All About It!

At-Home Objective: Use this activity to teach your child about the newspaper.

Activity: We learn a lot about the world from the newspaper. Pretend you are a newspaper reporter. Report about your community and share what you want the world to know about you and your neighbors.

The Neighborhood Gazette

GA1509

Walk in Their Shoes!

At-Home Objective: Use this activity to encourage your child's awareness of famous North Americans.

Activity: Choose a famous American and write a story all about this person and why you would or would not want to walk in his or her shoes.

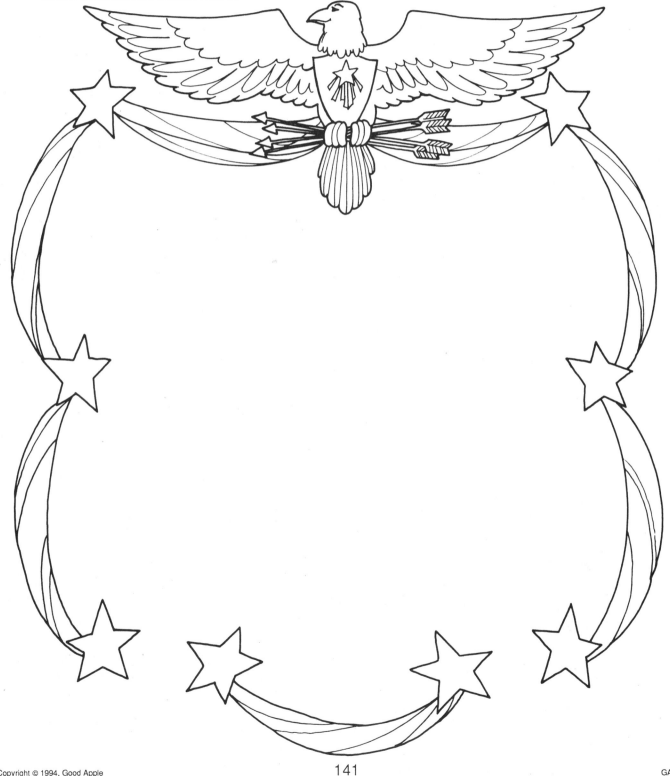

141

Happy Holidays!

At-Home Objective: Use this activity to teach your child about the holidays of different cultures around the world.

Activity: Investigate and research another special holiday that occurs in a different culture than yours. Complete the statements below once you've learned all about it.

The holiday I have learned about is _birth days_

Hallaween chrismis

The Forth of culy

Favorite foods during this holiday are _candys_

candycanes   punkinpie

Customs that are observed are _____

_____

_____

This holiday is most like _____

_____

_____

Here is how it is different. _____

_____

_____

GA1509

High-Flying Flag!

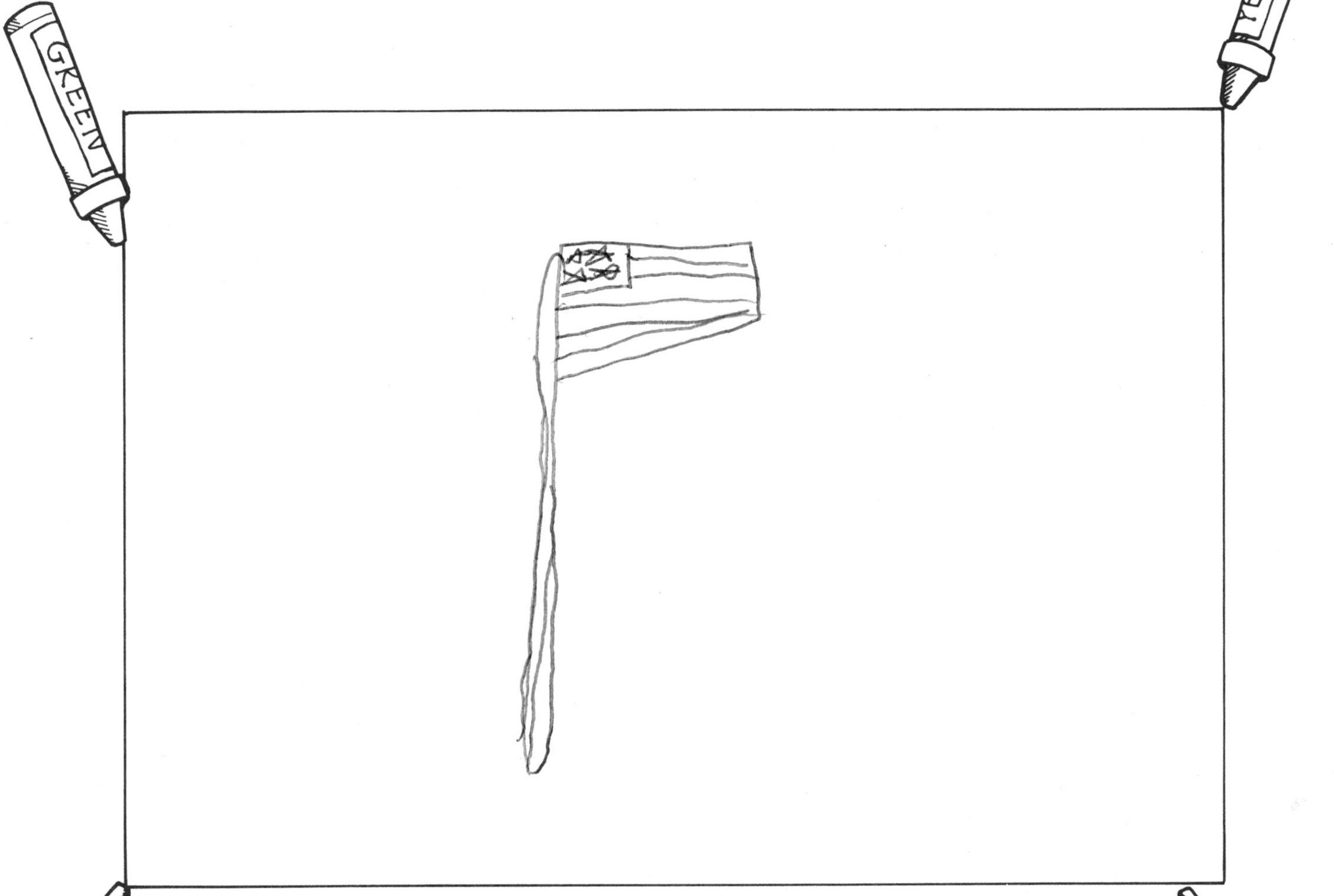

Describe your country's flag and explain what the symbols on the flag stand for.

_____

_____

_____

_____

_____

The Presidents

At-Home Objective: The United States celebrates two holidays to honor former Presidents, but there are many Presidents to honor.

Activity: Ask your child to name the current President of the United States and list or draw a picture of what he does all day. Talk about other things the President does.

GA1509

Independence Day

At-Home Objective: July 4th is a time of great celebration in the United States. Use it to teach your child a little history.

Activity: American colonial forefathers in the American colonies declared themselves independent of England on July 4, 1776. We celebrate this historic occasion in many ways. What are some things you can do because you live in a free country? Draw pictures of some of the things you can do because you live in a free country.

GA1509

Famous People, Famous Events

At-Home Objective: Many famous people and events are honored with holidays and celebrations. The calendar becomes a history lesson when you study it this way.

Activity: Look through the calendar. List all the people or events that are recognized. Did you find . . .

Canada Day?
The first United States President?
The man who discovered America?
The U.S. President during the Civil War?
A great civil rights leader?
Canadian Thanksgiving?

Pretend you are about to proclaim a new holiday. Who or what would you want to honor and why? Pick the date of the holiday and complete the calendar month for your holiday.

Sunday	Monday	Tuesday	Wednesday	Thursday	Friday	Saturday
					1	2
3	4	5	6	7	8	9
10	11	12	13	14	15	

GA1509

The White House

GA1509

2, 4, 6, 8! Who Do We Appreciate?

At-Home Objective:	We honor people in many ways. Recognizing the fact that the people who are on common objects are there for a reason leads to interesting learning.
Activity:	Place a penny, nickel, dime, quarter, and half-dollar on the table. Help your child identify the faces on each. Read about each person in the encyclopedia, and speculate on why that person was chosen.
	Ask your child to draw pictures of other ways people might be honored.

GA1509

Invent "ease"

GA1509

Team Up

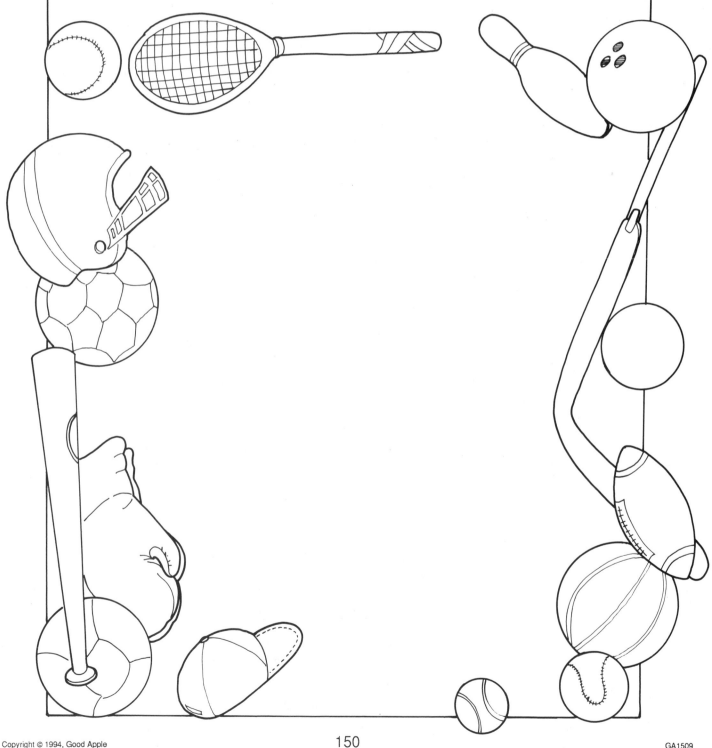

GA1509

Mr. Postman

At-Home Objective: Children love helping, and getting the mail is a favorite chore. Use the mail to talk about goods and services and the places the mail is delivered from.

Activity: Have your child get the mail from the mailbox. Look through the letters. Divide the mail into categories like bills, letters, and advertisements. Talk about the purposes of each. Have your child look at the return address on each envelope. How many different places are there? Write the return address of the place farthest from where you live in the box below.

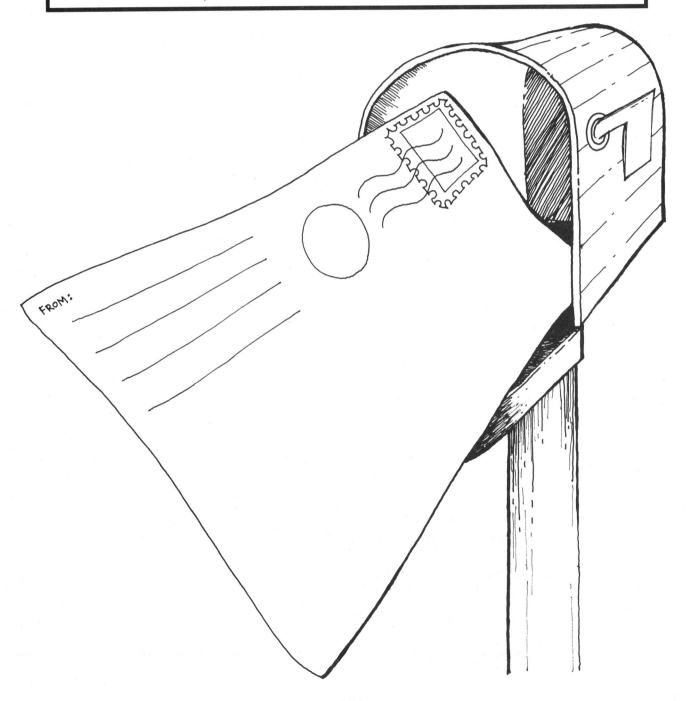

FROM:

Home Sweet Home

152

Check It Out!

At-Home Objective: Use this activity to encourage your child's awareness of his or her environment.

Activity: There are many ways that you can help protect our land. Here are some ideas to get you started. See how many you can add to the list.

☐ Do not litter.

☐ Recycle anything that can be recycled.

☐ Walk instead of riding in a car whenever you can.

☐ Use both sides of your paper.

☐ Think of new ideas for things you usually throw away.

☐ Reuse items instead of throwing them out.

GA1509

Endangered Animals

There are over one hundred animals on the list of endangered species. With this project you can teach your child that it is important to respect nature.

Activity:
It's important to take care of the earth and all its inhabitants. Cut out pictures of some of your favorite animals from magazines. Next write a letter to

The Office of Endangered Species
Fish and Wildlife
U.S. Department of the Interior
Washington, DC 20240

to find out the names of all the animals on the endangered species list.

GA1509

Cut Down on Trees

At-Home Objective: Paper is made of trees. We need to begin early to teach children to respect the environment.

Activity: Take a walk with your child and talk about how paper is made from trees. Have your child draw pictures of some things that are made from trees. Ask your child to guess how many pieces of paper the family uses in a week. Next keep a record of how many pieces of paper you use in two days by coloring in the pages you use in the graph below. Do you think you wasted any paper?

100
90
80
70
60
50
40
30
20
10

155

GA1509

Acid Rain

At-Home Objective: *Good citizenship* means "understanding the problems our country faces." Use this activity to teach your child about the environment.

Activity: Travel in the industrial part of your town. Do you see any dark wastes going into the sky? Acid rain is caused partially by burning coal or oil to make electricity. The gases float with the wind and dissolve in raindrops that erode buildings and kill trees and plants.

What kinds of pollution do you see as you travel through your town? What other kinds of trash do you see in your town? Add them to the picture.

GA1509

Pay Up

At-Home Objective:	Water is a precious commodity that shouldn't be wasted. Use these activities to begin teaching your child to respect the environment.
Activity:	Explain to your child that you have to pay for the water the family uses. Look at your water meter. Record your reading in the boxes on one circle below, and then two days later, read the meter again and record the reading on the second circle. What is the difference in the two amounts?

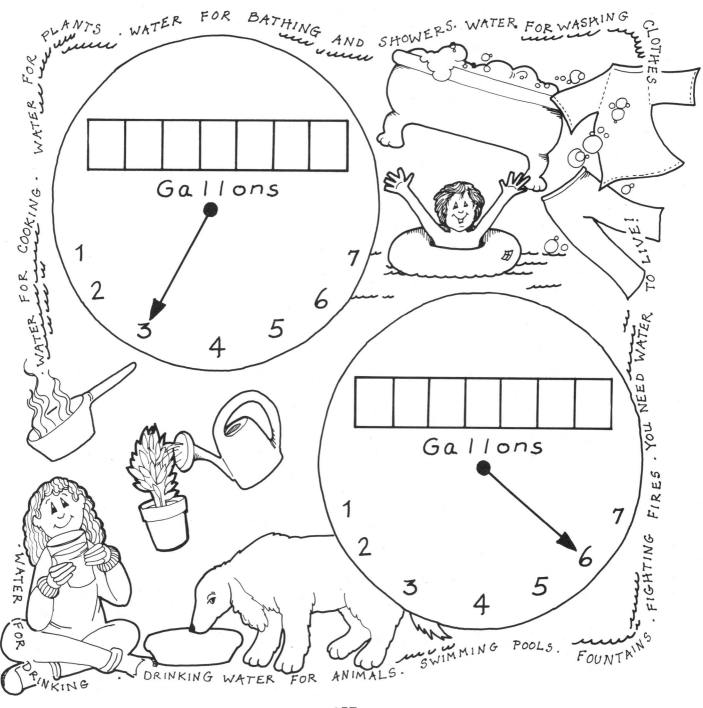

GA1509

Getting the
Lay of the Land